The
Power of
Storytelling

The Power of Storytelling

A Step-by-Step Guide to Dramatic Learning in K-12

Harriet Mason

CORWIN PRESS, INC.
A Sage Publications Company
Thousand Oaks, California

For information address:

Corwin Press, Inc.
SAGE Publications, Inc.
2455 Teller Road
Thousand Oaks, California 91320
E-mail: order@corwin.sagepub.com

SAGE Publications Ltd.
6 Bonhill Street
London EC2A 4PU
United Kingdom

SAGE Publications India Pvt. Ltd.
M-32 Market
Greater Kailash I
New Delhi 110 048 India

Printed in the United States of America

Library of Congress Cataloging-in-Publication Data

Mason, Harriet.
    The power of storytelling: A step-by-step guide to dramatic
learning in K-12 / Harriet Mason.
        p. cm.
    Includes bibliographical references.
    ISBN 0-8039-6413-7 (acid-free paper).—ISBN 0-8039-6414-5 (pbk. :
    acid-free paper)
    1. Storytelling. I. Title.
LB1042.M29   1996
372.64'2—dc20   95-50176

This book is printed on acid-free paper.

96   97   98   99   10   9   8   7   6   5   4   3   2   1

Corwin Press Production Editor: Tricia K. Bennett
Corwin Press Copy Editor: Gillian Dickens

Contents

Preface

In the past 10 years, there has been a resurgence of storytelling as a folk art and as an educational tool. Storytelling and creative dramatics are exciting and effective whole-language activities that make teaching experiential and relevant to the student. When stories are made part of the lesson plan, students remember and understand information better, and their interest and attention are held longer.

With the increased popularity and demonstrated success of the whole-language approach to teaching and with the national recommendations to incorporate arts into the curriculum instead of using outside artists, I have been asked repeatedly about ways teachers can use storytelling and dramatics in the classroom. This book was written to answer those questions. It contains more than 100 lesson-related whole-language activities for PK-12 classroom use, not only for language arts units but across the curriculum. These activities show how stories can be used to introduce a unit of study, to enrich it, and to follow it up while motivating students to create their own stories. Many examples and original stories that were generated by using these activities are included. Tables of grade-level guidelines are provided at the end of each chapter.

Chapter 1, "Introduction: Storytelling Across the Curriculum," gives many suggestions with examples for using storytelling in the classroom. Chapter 2, "Telling and Generating Stories," provides helpful information about telling stories and teaching storytelling. It gives a wealth of ideas for motivating students to create and tell their own stories and answers that age-old complaint, "I can't think of anything to write about." Chapter 3, "Integrating the Arts Into Storytelling," includes activities and examples of ways that storytelling can be used with the literary, visual, music, and movement arts. Chapter 4, "Working With Story Lines," includes lesson-related activities that teach the basics of storytelling and creative dramatics. Each activity lists a time estimate, a suggested grade level, a level of difficulty, and any preparation necessary. These are followed by specific comments and information, a step-by-step description of the procedure, some suggested variations, and helpful hints. Numerous examples and original stories are included throughout. Chapter 5, "Description and Characterization," includes activities that teach how to enrich and expand stories and creative dramatics through the use of description and point of view. Like Chapter 4 activities, these list time estimates, suggested grade levels, levels of difficulty, necessary preparation, specific comments, and information before each procedure is explained step-by-step. Suggestions for variations, helpful hints, examples, and original stories follow.

About the Author

Harriet Mason was a highly experienced presenter and teacher of story-telling for educators and mental health professionals up until her death in November 1995. She brought 40 years of counseling, 25 years of teaching, and 16 years of public speaking, acting, and storytelling experience to her workshops and performances. She had a B.S. in Education and an M.A. in Speech Pathology. She was also a licensed marriage, family, and child counselor. She told stories and taught storytelling to groups ranging in age from preschool to seniors and in ability from physically challenged to talented and gifted.

The author of *Every One a Storyteller* and *Telling Makes It So,* she also recorded several audiotapes of original personal stories. She conducted numerous seminars and in-services for schools and such organizations as Kaiser Foundation, Pacific Gateway Hospital and Counseling Center, Portland State University, Lewis and Clark College, and the International Reading Association and also lectured in Australia and New Zealand.

1

Introduction

Storytelling Across the Curriculum

Everyone loves a story. When stories are made part of the lesson plan, students remember and understand the information better, and their interest and attention are held longer. When they contribute to the story by helping to tell and/or create it, they experience Goodman's (1986) whole-language goals of choice, ownership, and relevance.

When we listen to a story, we enter into a special state of perception and receptivity. If the storytelling method involves class participation, that's even better. When students help a story to develop, they feel a proprietary interest in it and will be more likely to retell it to family and friends. I recently happened to meet a young man, now in 10th grade, who introduced himself as having had a class with me when he was in 7th grade. He still remembered the story we made up together and proceeded to tell it to every one present. He remembered it far better than I did.

When students hear their ideas recognized by the teacher and accepted by their classmates, they get a boost in self-confidence. They learn flexibility and teamwork in the cooperative creation of a story. Stories can be adapted to the students' abilities, experience, and level of maturity. They can tie in with special holidays and events or with units being studied. The effectiveness of stories is not limited to language arts subjects, as the activities in this book will demonstrate.

Math problems are little stories in and of themselves, of course. Sequencing, numbering, spatial relationships, memory training, and problem solving are learned by listening to stories.

Younger students enjoy cumulative stories in which objects are added or subtracted as the story progresses, and older students have their interest piqued when math is needed to solve a mystery. Stories about famous mathematicians and their discoveries will stimulate interest in the subject. Students can write stories about their efforts to understand a formula and their feelings about the struggle.

Stories can help students to see how important and relevant math can be. For example, exponents can be taught by the story of the merchant who, when told his price was too high, made a counteroffer: The customer could put one penny on the first square of a checkerboard and double the amount on each succeeding square. The customer agreed readily, much to his sorrow. By figuring out how much the customer had to pay, students have fun while learning the concept of exponential progression.

I once taught a grade-school class about decimals by telling them a story about two opposing armies that could choose their own numbers and weapons. The students armed the first force with a huge arsenal and a vast horde of soldiers. The second force had only one weapon: a gun that could shoot decimal points one at a time. Each time a decimal point was fired, depending on where the point landed, the enemy's resources were reduced by one placemarker, or 10%, which the students calculated. By the time the enemy was totally decimated, the students understood the base 10 number system and the relationship of decimals to percentages and fractions.

Stories about famous scientists and students' stories about their experiences can be used in units about science to stimulate interest. Stories can be told that raise scientific questions and explore possible solutions. They can motivate students to learn the principles and tools they will need to find other solutions. Natural disasters can be written about from the viewpoint of a survivor with the requirement, of course, that the story be researched and factually correct. Experimental procedure will be remembered better if it is taught in dramatized storytelling form from the viewpoint either of a participant or of someone who tries to discredit the study because its results are bad for business. Students can be taught about behavioral motivation, public masks, and private masks through point-of-view story activities. Skills necessary for scientific study are enhanced and developed by stories in general. They teach listening skills, evaluation, questioning, the ability to form a hypothesis and predict an outcome, problem solving, and teamwork.

History is in itself a narrative of past events. Stories make history and social studies memorable and interesting by allowing students to identify with the events being studied instead of having to learn a dull list of names and dates. Plots help to tie facts together and make important points more vivid.

Stories teach values and perpetuate culture and heritage. They can be retold and changed and told again. Stories can act as a springboard for follow-up activities involving reading, writing, art, and music. They can be written down and read silently or aloud. A student may want to learn more about the times and people in a story and will be motivated to read books about them. Stories told in class can be written down and illustrated. Letters can be written to characters in the stories. Music or poetry can be written for inclusion in the story or as a student's reaction to the story. A book of student-authored stories, which can be made and used for subsequent reading lessons, can be left as a legacy to the next incoming class or placed in the school library. To do this, students might want to learn bookbinding or papermaking, printing, typing, or calligraphy.

The four whole-language functions of speaking, listening, writing, and reading are natural components of storytelling activities. A fifth function is added when stories are dramatized. Many of the activities in this book use creative dramatics to give additional kinesthetic feedback to the student and facilitate experiential learning. I strongly suggest that classroom dramatic activities be improvised and not performed from a ready-made, memorized script. A script makes Goodman's goals of choice, ownership, and relevance difficult to achieve.

Even if the students have chosen their roles, unless they have participated in creating the character and the language, they will feel little ownership or relevance to the words they speak. The professional actor's job is to make the author's language seem relevant and authentic; the beginning student has enough other things to worry about. Even when a script is student generated, I recommend that it consist of only a sketchy scenario of important points to be made, with the students improvising the actual language each time they rehearse or present it.

There are other important advantages of improvisation over memorization: First and foremost, there are no mistakes, so everyone is assured of success in both the use of language and performance. Each student knows what needs to happen and shares the responsibility to present the necessary information, further the plot, and support his or her fellow actors to help them look good. If a student doesn't give a needed response, another will supply it in context so that it looks as if it were supposed to happen that way. Not only are listening skills and teamwork enhanced by improvised dramatics, but creativity and self-confidence also are increased. There is no better book on how to teach improvisation to students than Viola Spolin's (1963) much-used text. She gives a problem-solving, theater game approach to teaching. When doing some of the dramatics activities, students might be motivated to devise and use costumes, props, scenery, and makeup, although they are not necessary for the activities to be effective.

Stories are excellent ways to facilitate group acceptance of outsiders, such as students who are new, foreign, members of minority groups, or physically or emotionally challenged. For example, the teacher can help the class make up a story in which all the power (magic) words are in the language of the new foreign student. Or the story could be an adventure in which the entire class goes to a foreign land and will need the new student to translate for them and keep them out of trouble. Making a foreign student the hero of the story can help to make classmates' attitudes more accepting toward him or her.

Another good way to help your students understand what it is like to come to a foreign land is to divide the students into two groups and instruct one of the groups to speak only nonsense syllables. Have each student take a turn asking directions from the opposite group. Some will be asking in English and getting nonsense in return while others will be speaking nonsense to English-speaking people who won't understand them. Some may be able to make themselves understood by using gestures. Whatever happens, students should gain some insight into the frustrations of students who speak little English. There are many excellent stories dealing with the integration of outsiders. The teacher could tell one of these stories to the class, with class discussion afterward. Students could share anecdotes about their own heritage. They also could be encouraged to ask their families for stories about the past that would be shared. A story incorporating foreign words could be told and used to introduce a unit on that country.

Very special students can benefit greatly from storytelling. We all know learning disabled children who have learned to associate reading and writing with frustration and failure. These students can experience success with storytelling, especially when their contributions to a group storybuilding are used without them having to be responsible for the entire story. This type of shared responsibility is far less threatening and stressful, so the student feels less anxiety and less pressure to perform.

Once, during a school residency, I was using a group storybuilding technique with a second-grade class. The special education teacher asked if Joey could observe. He was an 8-year-old boy with severe cerebral palsy who was restrained in a padded wheelchair to prevent him from injuring himself. The teacher said that Joey would understand the story but would not be able to contribute because he had no voluntary muscle control and therefore could not make any purposeful sounds. I told Joey I was glad he was there. There was no answering movement or eye contact to show that he had heard me.

I began the story and quickly took the students to a magical land and presented them with a series of problems to solve. At one point in the story, they were imprisoned in a mountain and were searching for a way to escape. At that point, Joey made an involuntary sound. I repeated the sound and said, "That's it! That's the magic sound." I had the students use Joey's "sound" to get out of the mountain and thanked Joey for rescuing them.

As the story progressed, the boy's random movements increased, and he began making the sound more often. Each time he made it, I had something magical occur in the story. By the end of the story, Joey was able to make the sound purposefully whenever I said, "And Joey made the magic sound . . ." This was an important achievement for him, because the making of intentional sound is one of the first steps in learning to speak. Just as important was the acceptance and importance that his peers gave him and the empowerment he felt as he contributed a pivotal part of the story.

In summation, stories can introduce, enrich, and provide follow-up for classroom units across the curriculum. I feel that stories are the best tools to stimulate imagination and creativity and impel students to learn. I hope this book is not only useful to you but enjoyable as well.

2

Telling and Generating Stories

Storytelling, by itself, is a valuable activity even when it is not being used as part of a unit of study. It is a natural bridge to reading and writing. Storytelling is a folk art, a tradition, and an entertainment. In these times, when children are losing the ability to abstract, create, and imagine, when children are being taught by the media to honor mediocrity, and when children are becoming more and more passive, storytelling should be part of every language arts program.

Stories perpetuate tradition, are a socialization instrument, and introduce new ideas. They develop empathy and the ability to laugh at oneself, and they link the known to the unknown. They are a source of security and continuity and attune the ear to language flow, imagery, and speech rhythms. They build the language skills of repetition, recognition, rhyme, counting, time sense, and sequencing in a meaningful and relevant context.

To introduce storytelling to the classroom, you, the teacher, should first tell a story to the class. There are many times when reading to your students from a book is appropriate, but for this introductory storytelling activity, please do not read the story to them. No matter how well you read or how often you look up, the book will be a physical barrier between you and your students. Even if you share the pictures with them, the barrier is still there, and you will have to interrupt the narrative flow to show the pictures. By telling the story to the class, you provide a model for them, and you introduce storytelling in a nonthreatening situation in which student participation is mostly passive.

You don't have to be polished and professional. In fact, it may be better if you're not, because you are modeling for your class. If there is too much perceived difference between what they see and what they think they can learn to do, your students will be less likely to risk trying something new. A hero is someone whose acts we admire, about whom we can say, "I can learn to do that"; an idol is someone about whom we say, "I can never do that, so there's no point in trying." We can try to be like a hero; all we can do with an idol is try to tear it down.

So if your story effort is not perfect, you can be comfortable knowing that you are a hero-model for your students and not an idol that can discourage effort and risk.

Choosing a Story to Tell

Stories to tell can be found everywhere and anywhere. Books, movies, television shows, plays, newspapers, comic strips, nursery rhymes, fairy tales, tall tales, and urban legends are all stories you can retell. Or you can take ideas from them and use them in a story of your own. You can retell reminiscences, oral histories, remembered stories from your own childhood, ghost stories, and dreams. You can use pictures and other artwork, poetry, music, and units being studied. The list is truly inexhaustible. There are many excellent books in the library that contain stories for retelling. A partial list of "Stories for Retelling" may be found at the end of this chapter.

Remember that happy endings provide closure; unhappy endings do the opposite and keep the student thinking about the story. Find a story that you really like and read through it enough times to familiarize yourself with it. Do not memorize it. Memorized pieces keep the teller aloof from the audience. The speaker's anxiety about forgetting and the stilted lines make the audience restless and uncomfortable.

There are many ways to remember a story. Often, storytellers make an outline or use file cards in sequence for the key points. Others draw a cartoon strip or a story map. Use whatever works for you. Some storytellers make a tape recording of the story and listen to it over and over again until they've learned it. Then it's a good idea to tell your learned story into a tape recorder or to a live audience, if you have a captive one at home. Either method will give you needed practice and feedback on how you sound.

Before choosing a story, the teacher should consider the audience's age, experience, maturity, and abilities. Some school districts are opposed to fairy tales or any stories about spirits, ghosts, or magic. Certain religious groups request that stories about holidays such as Christmas, Halloween, and so on not be told. I leave such political decisions to your own discretion.

For K-2 children, simple story lines with few or no subplots and lots of repetition are best. Repetition trains memory and the ability to forecast, both of which provide familiarity and security. For this age, use simple characters who behave in predictable ways instead of fully developed three-dimensional characters. Keep motivation simple; the hero does good things, and the villain is bad. Settings should be established quickly for the younger group without much description. Begin the action immediately after introducing the characters and setting. For this age, time moves quickly, often only needing the words "Years passed."

For older children, more time can be spent on description and character development. Motivation becomes important, and moral issues can be introduced. Several subplots and even some ambiguity are appropriate.

The following story was told to an advanced second-grade class and later written down. In this story, as in many of the group stories I facilitate, I put the entire class into the story. When I was telling the story, I asked the students to problem solve how the children in the basement might be rescued. One of them suggested that they pool their money to buy a rope, and all agreed except a girl named Heather. So I put that into the story.

Story: The Magic Shop

The children in the second grade were going to visit a Magic Store. They were excited because they each had one dollar to spend on anything they wanted. When the class got to the Magic Store, they gave their money to their teacher to hold for them.

The children explored the shop to see what they wanted to buy. There were so many wonderful things to see and some scary things, too.

There was a door with a sign that read "Do Not Enter." I'm sorry to tell you that some of the children opened that door and walked into a little closet. They fell through a trap door and landed in the basement. They started yelling for help.

The children upstairs heard them and ran to see what had happened. They saw their classmates far below with no stairs or ladder to climb.

"I've got an idea," said one of the children upstairs. "We'll ask the teacher to put all our money together and buy a rope to pull them up." The children thought that was a good idea—all except one. Heather did not want her dollar used to buy rope. So their teacher had only 10 dollars to buy the rope, which cost 11 dollars. The teacher added a dollar of her own and bought the rope.

The children dropped the rope down to the trapped children. Heather jumped down to help them climb faster. Soon all the children were rescued, and it was Heather's turn. Cody pulled up the rope before Heather could grab it. Cody said, "You can't use the rope because you didn't pay for it."

Heather didn't know what to do. She said, "I'm sorry. I wish now I had given my dollar, too." Cody threw the rope down and Heather climbed out. Then Heather spent her dollar on candy and shared it with everyone.

The End

The resolution and retribution in this story were contributed by the students. They overlooked the fact that Heather actually did physically help to rescue her classmates. During the poststory discussion, we dealt with issues of fairness, sharing, and teamwork.

Ritual Beginnings and Endings

Communication and interaction are improved when students are seated in a circle or a semicircle instead of behind one another in rows. Many stories begin with ritual words or gestures to encourage an anticipatory mind-set. Can you sense the change in your attitude and awareness when you read "Once upon a time . . ."? You become more relaxed, more receptive.

Everyone can remember a traditional favorite beginning. Here is a small sample from different cultures:

Long ago, in a kingdom far away . . .

Now, it came to pass . . .

This is a story about . . .

There was once, in old times, and in old times it was . . . (Ireland)

More years ago than you can tell me and twice as many as I can tell you . . . (Ireland)

Once upon a time and a very good time it was, tho' it was neither in my time nor in your time nor in anyone else's time . . . (England)

In a certain kingdom, in a certain land, in a certain village, there lived . . . (Russia)

In the beginning, when the world was new . . . (Maidu, California)

At the time when men and animals were all the same and spoke in the same tongue . . . (Navajo, Arizona)

In Haiti, a would-be storyteller will say "Crick." If someone answers "Crack," that signals the group's confidence in the storyteller, and everyone settles down to hear the story. If no one answers "Crack," the storyteller remains silent for he or she has received no invitation to proceed.

You and your class can experiment with creating your own story beginnings and share them. How about "Once upon an itchy afternoon . . ." or "Many years and tears ago . . ."?

A special candle can be lit or a ritual chant spoken to signal the beginning of a storytelling and to begin the story mind-set. Instructing children to "put on their listening hat" is the same type of signal. A special story shawl also can be worn, or a special tune can be played. Some classrooms have a story corner or story mats so that going to a special place becomes part of the beginning ritual.

Choosing the story to be told can be part of the beginning ritual. Story shirts, vests, or aprons worn by the storyteller contain many pockets. Inside the pockets are small objects, written phrases, or titles. By choosing a pocket, the students select the story. Verna Aardema (1960), a teller of African tales, says she met a storyteller in West Africa who wore a story hat from which objects such as a spider, skull, or various animals dangled on strings attached to the brim. Each object represented a story in his repertoire, and his listeners selected the story they wanted by pointing to the appropriate object.

There is also a ritual ending to stories, signaling that it's time to return to the real world. Some traditional favorites include the following:

> . . . and they all lived happily ever after.
> . . . and if they didn't live happily ever after, that's nothing to do with you or me. (England)
> This was given to me by my teacher and I give it you. (Indian)
> Billy Ben. My story end. (Bahamas)
> Snip, snap, snout. This tale's told out. (Germany)
> No matter whether it is told or not, that's the way it happened. (Japan)
> . . . and that's the end of that.
> . . . and if they haven't moved, they live there still.
> May you take it and may the next one tell it better. (Ireland)
> Ho! (Native American)

Tools for Storytelling

There are many tools that storytellers use to "sell" their stories.

Eye contact is important. It pulls the listener into the story and changes an aloof performance into a personal communication. Variation in delivery, such as in pace or volume, spices up a story and changes moods. If you gradually increase the pace, it will make a scary story more frightening. If you speak quietly, it will either build suspense or soothe the listeners, depending on the context.

Timing can greatly affect the listeners. For example, " . . . and out of the thick bushes came [pause] . . . a little girl" (let your voice show surprise), or " . . . [pause] an ogre" (let your voice show dismay or fear). Please don't use phony cheerfulness. It is condescending, and the response to that tone of voice is usually negative, disruptive, or regressive.

Character voices or dialects add color to a story, but if they don't come easily, forget them. Your class will sense your uncertainty and discomfort, which will make them uncomfortable. Even worse, if some of your students belong to the ethnic group whose accent you are attempting, they may infer condescension where none is intended. Nonverbal techniques, such as posture, gesture, and facial expression add richness to your story.

The idea of *telling* a story instead of reading it may be scary to contemplate. Realizing that, I have made a partial list of "Stories for Retelling" that you will find at the end of this chapter. Any of these will help you feel more confident and competent. But—and this is a big *but*—if you like the story you are telling, and you want to tell it, you don't have to worry about techniques. Concentrate on the story instead of yourself, and your enjoyment will be contagious. Gestures, facial expression, voice, and timing will take care of themselves and will be appropriate. I urge you to take the risk. After all, you, as teacher, are the model for your students, and you will be asking them to risk also. Many of the activities in this book involve the creation of original stories, and often you will be acting as facilitator. You gradually can move into the facilitation of group story-building and creative dramatics with the continuum of class involvement that follows.

Having selected and told your first story, gradually increase class participation in the storytelling. You could teach your students a gesture, rhyme, and/or phrase to add to the story when appropriate, such as shaking a forefinger or saying, "No, no, Joe, don't go!" Younger children especially enjoy rhymes and songs, which they learn and remember easily. Riddles and jokes also can be incorporated into a story.

Your students will enjoy adding sound effects, such as wind blowing, doors creaking, popcorn popping, and so on. In fact, sound effects are so much fun to make that a ghost story loses its scariness when told in this manner.

You can ask the class to tell what a character took on a picnic or ask for the ingredients of a magic brew. You can stop the story and ask, "What do you think he had for lunch?" or "Would you go in?" The more student involvement in the story, the more closely your students will listen to it and the more ownership they will feel.

You can ask the students to retell the story in their own words. They can draw or paint a picture of their favorite part of the story and use their pictures as memory aids when retelling the story. These pictures can be arranged in sequence, with each artist contributing his or her part of the story. Not only does this activity train listening skills and memory, it also teaches sequencing, story construction, and teamwork.

The students can retell your story from another character's point of view. Although they still are not responsible for the story line, they will be taking more initiative for characterization and dialogue. This activity teaches empathy and paves the way for acceptance of differences and intercultural understanding and appreciation.

They can write down the story they have retold and read it aloud or listen to another student read it to the class. Student stories can be compiled into a book, perhaps with illustrations.

So far, the teacher has provided the story line and has involved the students in description and characterization. The next step is to give the students gradually increasing responsibility for the story line. This is best begun with a group activity, and the easiest place to start is with the ending of a story. "How do you think the party turned out?" or "How do you think they got away?" After all suggestions have been heard, have the students choose their favorite one and use it to retell the story. Then the stories can be written, if desired. An art activity can be incorporated, either as a memory aid for retelling or to illustrate the written story.

This done, the students are ready to take even more responsibility for the plot. The teacher will provide the characters, setting, and quest or theme, and the students will contribute the conflict and resolution. This can be either a group or individual activity, and writing and art can be incorporated as previously described. Telling or writing their own stories without suggestions from the teacher or the group is the last step in the hierarchy of student responsibility for the story line. All that remains to teach them is how to use description and characterization.

Generating Stories

After telling your story to the class, you and they might feel more comfortable "warming up" to storytelling before plunging right into some of the more structured activities. These warm-ups should generate story starters, which will take care of the age-old complaint, "I don't know what to tell (write) about" and will get the student used to telling stories in front of a group.

Tongue twisters like "Peter Piper picked a peck of pickled peppers" or "How much wood would a woodchuck chuck . . . ?" and songs such as *Bingo* or *On Top of Spaghetti* are fun to do but usually do not lead to storytelling ideas. Instead, I prefer to get the group members talking about themselves, because an excellent source of material for student stories is the students themselves and their families.

Not only is the information readily available to them, but we are telling the students that they are worth writing about, that they're interesting people, and that their thoughts and feelings are important. Relevance and ownership are ensured when the students tell and write about themselves and their experiences. Introductions are a great way to get things started.

Me, Myself, and Others

Introduction. Have students take turns giving their names and telling something interesting about themselves.

Proxy Introduction. Have students introduce themselves to the class as someone important in their lives might talk about them.

Interview. Have students pair off and tell one another about themselves. You can provide a list of questions for them to ask one another, or you could have the class generate a list. After each student has had a turn, bring everyone together and have partners introduce one another to the class, telling what they have learned about their partners.

Journal. Have your students keep a diary or journal for an assigned time period, including not only what they did and what happened but also their feelings, fears, and hopes. Assure them that they won't have to show their journals to anyone; these journals are private and won't be handed in. At the end of the assigned period, have them review their own journals. They can take one of the entries and expand it into a story, or they can change any part of it to make a different story. They can write in either first or third person. Instead of a story, they can write a song or a poem about what they have written in the journal.

Autobiography. Have your students write an autobiography, including the events in their families' lives that have affected them. For example, why did the family come to this city? What involvement do the grandparents have? In these days of nontraditional families that include single parents, multiple parents, nonparental caretakers, and so on, sharing these autobiographies in class might lead to better understanding and tolerance.

Forecast. Have your students imagine where they will be in 10 years and what they will be doing.

Nightmares. Lead a discussion about nightmares. If your students can't remember one or don't want to talk about ones that they've had, they can talk about one they've heard or make up one. Have them write a story about the dream, changing the ending so that it comes out all right.

Memories. Ask your students to talk about childhood memories, being sure to include recollections of smells, sounds, or other sensations. Ask them to write a story about a childhood memory, being sure to incorporate sensory recollections.

Scary Things. Talk about scary things with your students. What objects or symbols are scary? What books, movies, or television shows are scary? What makes a scary story fun? (Scary stories are fun when you know you are safe, either because you are only reading or watching them or because you know you will escape or triumph.) Talk about the role of surprise and suspense in scary stories. Have your students write a scary story.

It is important to let your students know they don't have to talk about painful or frightening things that happened to them. After all, you are a teacher, not a counselor (although the lines do blur at times), and the classroom is not an appropriate place for emotional outbursts, especially assignment-generated ones. Give your students the option of writing about a scary movie or television show they saw or of creating a story with fictional characters. That should give them enough distance from their own fears to allow them to do the assignment.

If your students choose to write about their own experiences, suggest that because this is a story, they can change any event or choices to make the story end differently than it did in real life, if they want to.

Funny Things. Ask your students what was the funniest thing that ever happened to them or to one of their family members. (What made it funny? Who were the people involved? How did they act? Did they think it was funny at the time?) Ask your students to write a story about a funny incident and then to share it with the class. If the class does not find it humorous, discuss ways it could be changed to make the story sound funnier.

Obituary. Ask your students to write their own obituary, telling how old they were when they died, the cause of death, lifetime accomplishments, and survivors. Ask them to describe the funeral and who was there.

Likes and Dislikes. Likes and dislikes, preferences, and choices make spirited class discussions, which then can be developed into stories. Have

TABLE 2.1 Grade-Level Guidelines: Me, Myself, and Others

	K-12	PK-2	3-5	6-12
Introduction	X			
Proxy Introduction	X			
Interview	X			
Journal			X	X
Autobiography			X	X
Forecast			X	X
Nightmares	X			
Memories	X			
Scary Things	X			
Funny Things	X			
Obituary			X	X
Likes and Dislikes	X			
Strange Foods	X			
Homes	X			
Magical Creatures	X			
Magical Objects	X			

a class discussion about food likes and dislikes. Ask your students to write a story about what would happen if the only food they could get was the one they hated most, telling how they got in that situation and what they did about it.

Strange Foods. Have a class discussion about the strange foods that are eaten in other parts of the world, such as chocolate-covered ants, fried snake, or grubs. Ask your students which they would rather eat. Have them write a story about visiting a foreign land and being served a strange dish. Alternatively, discuss foods that we eat that other people might consider weird and have your students write a story about a foreigner (or extraterrestrial) dealing with our food.

Homes. Have a class discussion about the different places that people live and their different dwellings, such as trailers, apartments, palaces, igloos, tepees, or caves. Ask your students where they would rather live. Have them write a story about how their lives would be changed if they lived in a totally different place, in a different lifestyle.

Magical Creatures. Have a class discussion about magical creatures, such as dragons, ghosts, or magic fish. Ask your students which they would rather be. Have them write a story about either being or meeting a magical creature.

Magical Objects. Have a class discussion about magical objects, such as seven-league boots, a cloak of invisibility, or a purse that always has money in it, no matter how much is taken out. Ask your students which they would rather have. Have them write a story about a magical object.

Oral Histories

Oral histories are an excellent source for stories and a valuable link to the past. They tie in beautifully with social studies units and with multicultural studies.

The techniques of collecting these histories range in complexity from simply recording unstructured reminiscences, to informal interviewing, to preparing a list of questions for the speaker to answer. Once recorded, the histories can be used in several projects. Some examples follow.

Childhood. Your students can write a story about their grandmother or grandfather's childhood. They may have to ask their grandparents for additional details, such as what their house looked like, where they slept, what they wore, what they ate, what kind of chores they did, and anything else needed for the story. If grandparents are not available, neighbors, aunts and uncles, or members of a senior center make good substitutes. There have been some wonderful oral history projects done with selected populations, such as in a neighborhood or in a retirement home. These projects have not only preserved traditions and memories but also have brought children and older citizens together in contact that enriches and teaches both groups.

Make a Play. Your students can transcribe the obtained oral histories into written form and then put them into play form, asking for any additional information they might need from the people giving the histories. Students can research the period in the library for appropriate costumes and props and then perform the play. Costumes and props need not be used but should be researched anyway.

TABLE 2.2 Grade-Level Guidelines: Oral Histories

	K-12	PK-2	3-5	6-12
Childhood			X	X
Make a Play				X
Photo Album				X
Slide Show				X

Photo Album. Have your students ask for old photographs and make an album, matching quotes from the oral histories they have recorded with the appropriate pictures. Have them ask for anecdotes about the people in the photographs and include those also. Present the album to the person who gave the oral history.

Slide Show. Help your students make a slide show of old photographs. You can get additional pictures from the Historical Society in Washington, D.C. (1307 New Hampshire Ave. NW, Washington, D.C. 20036) if needed. Recorded oral histories can be used as a voice-over narrative for the show.

Tall Tales

Lies and half-truths make great story starters. An invitation to bend the truth just naturally stimulates the imagination. Fish stories and other whoppers belong in this category, as do tall tales.

Two Truths and a Lie. This activity is a favorite with many storytellers. The students take turns telling three things about themselves, only two of which are actually true. Then the class votes as to which was the lie.

Apple Tree. This activity is done by so many teachers and tellers, it's hard to know who started it. In my version, the class begins by using a poem to designate which student is to tell a story, much as in *Eeny Meeny Myney Mo.* The students chant,

As I climbed up the apple tree
All the apples fell on me.
Apple pudding, apple pie,
Did you ever tell a lie?

TABLE 2.3 Grade-Level Guidelines: Tall Tales

	K-12	PK-2	3-5	6-12
Two Truths and a Lie	X			
Apple Tree		X	X	
Liar's Contest			X	X

The designated student then tells a story, which may or may not be true. Then the students vote "thumbs-up" or "thumbs-down" as to whether they think the story is true or false. The student-teller then has a choice whether to reveal the truth about the story.

Then the class chants again, with the student who just told a story pointing to each student in turn until the chant ends and the next teller is chosen.

This activity can be much more than just a warm-up. You can choose a theme, such as animals, eating, or baseball, and all the stories will be about that subject.

Liar's Contest. Hold a liar's contest. The student who tells the most outrageous and entertaining story wins. The stories can be written down and collected in a book. If possible, the contest can be videotaped.

Folktales

Folktales are wonderful for generating story ideas. They include fables, parables and allegories, fairy tales, myths and legends, tall tales and fish stories, ghost stories, and urban legends. Distinctions between these terms are blurred, and many are used interchangeably (see Glossary).

Many cultures have similar stories; for example, "The Emperor's New Clothes," "The Fox and the Crow," "Echo and Narcissus," and "Crow and Octopus Woman" all have to do with vanity. For that matter, every culture has a Cinderella story, including African, Japanese, Chinese, and European versions. But whether her name is Ashputtel (Germany), Cap O'Rushes (England), Mead Moondaughter (Iceland), Zezolla (Italy), or Turkey Girl (Native American), the story is virtually the same.

Myths symbolize fundamental truths within societies; therefore parallel and similar stories can be found in many cultures, for example, creation myths. Virginia Hamilton (1988) has collected these in her excellent book, *In the Beginning: Creation Stories From Around the World.*

Many legends about folk heroes are based in fact. John Henry, Buffalo Bill Cody, and Daniel Boone are examples of American historical figures who have had many fictional adventures attributed to them in addition to their real-life exploits. There is controversy over whether Robin Hood or King Arthur ever lived, but that has not affected the popularity their stories still enjoy.

Tall tales, like those about Paul Bunyan and Pecos Bill, are legends that don't pretend to be based on fact, although they are told as if the storyteller believes they really happened. Their wild exaggerations are delightful. Sometimes, fanciful explanations are given for natural phenomena. For example, Paul Bunyan straightened out a winding river so he could send his logs downstream, and Pecos Bill dug the Rio Grande River while trying to break his bucking horse, "Widow Maker."

Urban legends aren't true, even though many people are certain they really happened. Some people believe that grown alligators live in the New York sewers. They will tell you very earnestly that hundreds of people brought baby alligators back as souvenirs from their Florida vacations. Later, they tired of them and flushed them down into the sewer system, where they flourished and grew to a very large size. Daily inspections by the city have never revealed a single alligator, but the legend persists.

Almost everyone knows some version of the ghostly hitchhiker: A young girl dressed in old-fashioned clothes is picked up on a lonely country road and given a ride to a house she points out. She gets out of the car, leaving behind her wrap, and goes into the house. When the driver discovers the wrap and goes back to give it to her, the occupants of the house tell him that the girl died years ago on that same country road where she just appeared.

Almost identical urban legends show up in all parts of the world. They have been gathered and printed in collections (Brunvand, 1981, 1984, 1989).

Ghost stories are great fun. Whenever I want to draw and hold a crowd at storytelling performances, I announce that I am going to tell a ghost story. The response is immediate and enthusiastic, and I think the adults are even more eager than the children.

Folktales of all kinds make excellent story starters and lead to whole-language activities. Some suggested activities follow.

Allegories. Fables, parables, and other allegories can be read and discussed in class. When the second underlying meaning is identified, ask your students to tell other stories they know that illustrate the same moral or spiritual value. Ask them to write their own original allegory illustrating the maxim. These stories can be shared with the class and/or collected into a book that can be used for subsequent language lessons.

Updated Tales. Folktales can be updated and given a modern location with present-day characters. For example, in the story of "Henny Penny," Henny could be announcing the imminent end of the world. As she gathers believers, they all sell or give their property to "Mr. Fox," who offers them safety in a spaceship that will take them off the planet.

Similarities. Compare stories on similar themes from other cultures. By realizing our similarities, rather than our differences, we build intercultural understanding and communication. Two excellent resources group stories by theme (Ireland, 1989; Yaakov & Greenfieldt, 1991).

Myths. Ask your students to bring to class a myth from their own cultural background or from one they want to know more about. Share the stories in class. Make a book of the collected myths with illustrations done by the students.

Historical Figures. Read and discuss a story about a folk hero who was actually a historical figure. (When did the hero live? What was the political and economic situation of that time?) Ask your students to compare the story with a history text and see if they can find where fact became fiction. Have them write a story about the folk hero and share it with the class. Collect all the student stories about the same hero and make a book of them.

Create a Hero. Ask your students to create a folk hero and write a story about him or her, making up a past history and a philosophy of life. (Does he or she fight injustice? Protect the poor? Have an ability to work hard? Show devotion to the job?) Remind your students to show the hero's characteristics, both physical and mental, in the story.

Ghost Stories. Invite your students to share ghost stories. If the situation allows, set the scene. Darken the room and sit on the floor around an imaginary campfire.

TABLE 2.4 Grade-Level Guidelines: Folktales

	K-12	PK-2	3-5	6-12
Allegories				X
Updated Tales			X	X
Similarities			X	X
Myths			X	X
Historical Figures			X	X
Create a Hero			X	X
Ghost Stories	X			
Urban Legends			X	X

Urban Legends. Read some urban legends to the class. Have students share some that they know. Have your students make up their own urban legend—something that sounds plausible but has no basis in fact. Collect student-generated urban legends and put them into a book.

Chance

The use of random choice can be a good story-starting device. Characters, places, obstacles, and so on can be written on slips of paper and placed in a container. The student draws one or more slips from the container and makes a story from them. This adds excitement to the activity and teaches flexibility. It also builds self-confidence, because students learn to trust their abilities to "think on their feet." Pictures, artifacts, and other objects also can be used in this way.

Many Round Robin activities use the element of chance (see Pocket Robin, Surprise Robin, and Touchie-Feelie Robin in Chapter 4).

What-Ifs

What-ifs are also excellent story starters. What if you opened the refrigerator and saw a three-inch bear trying to climb the milk carton? What if you reached into your closet and your jacket sleeve slapped your hand? What if you could only say the opposite of what you meant? The teacher has to give only a few suggestions before the class starts enthusiastically contributing their own what-ifs.

Stories for Retelling

Botkin, B. A. (1976). *A treasury of American folklore.* New York: Crown.

Chase, R. (1948). *Grandfather tales.* Boston: Houghton Mifflin.

Cole, J. (1982). *Best-loved folktales of the world.* New York: Anchor.

DeSpain, P. (1990). *Twenty-two splendid tales to tell.* Seattle, WA: Merrill Court.

Erdoes, R., & Ortiz, A. (1984). *American Indian myths and legends.* New York: Pantheon.

Hamilton, V. (1985). *The people could fly.* New York: Knopf.

MacDonald, M. R. (1986). *Twenty tellable tales.* New York: Wilson.

Schram, P. (1987). *Jewish stories: One generation tells another.* Northvale, NJ: Jason Aronson.

Schwartz, A. (1981). *Scary stories to tell in the dark.* New York: Lippincott.

Wolkstein, D. (1980). *The magic orange tree and other Haitian folktales.* New York: Schocken.

Yolen, J. (1986). *Favorite folktales from around the world.* New York: Pantheon.

Telling the Story

Baker, A., & Green, E. (1987). *Storytelling art and technique.* New York: Bowker.

Hutchinson, D. (1985). *Storytelling tips.* Lincoln, NE: Foundation Books.

Livo, N., & Reitz, S. (1986). *Storytelling process and practice.* Littleton, CO: Libraries Unlimited.

Maguire, J. (1985). *Creative storytelling: Choosing, inventing and sharing tales for children.* New York: McGraw-Hill.

Moore, R. (1991). *Awakening the hidden storyteller.* Boston: Shambala.

Sawyer, R. (1962). *The way of the storyteller.* New York: Viking.

3

Integrating the Arts Into Storytelling

Literary and visual arts, music, and dance enrich our lives as well as our stories. The arts can be an integral part of the story, such as the couplet used in "Rapunzel": "Rapunzel, Rapunzel, let down your hair, So I may climb without a stair." Or they can illustrate and enrich, as do Rackham's paintings for Barrie's (1980) *Peter Pan in Kensington Gardens.* Art can teach us and help us to recall what we've learned. We all remember how the music and rhymes of the *ABC Song* helped us to learn the alphabet and how *Frere Jacques* taught us all a few French words. Audiences can participate in the storytelling through such artistic expressions as music, chants, sound effects, gestures, dance, and costumes. In addition, audio- and videotapes can be used as a way to preserve stories, as a teaching tool, and as an aid in rehearsal.

Besides illustrating stories and giving them added dimension and color, the arts can help a story to develop and unfold. They can be used to introduce storytelling activities and actually engender the ideas for stories. Used as story starters, the arts act as a springboard for plot ideas, setting, characterization, and further creativity. Finally, the arts can be used in follow-up projects to stories after they have been told or written.

Chapters 4 and 5 contain many suggestions for the use of the arts in specific story games, and the following are some additional suggestions for integrating the arts into storytelling activities:

Literary Arts

The literary arts include written stories, plays, and poetry. Storytelling motivates students to read books about the subject of the story they have heard, and reading books leads to storytelling and writing activities.

Books

There are so many stories in print, and more are being written every day. No matter what subject you are teaching or what social and emotional issue you wish to address, you can easily find a book about it with vocabulary appropriate for your students' grade level.

There are pros and cons about reading aloud to your class rather than telling the story to them. You lose the immediacy and intimacy of spontaneous communication, but you gain the security that comes with using prepared material. When you read aloud, you don't have to worry about leaving something out, and you don't have to search for the right words to say.

The advantages of reading aloud to your class include the following:

1. Everyone hears the words at the same time, and discussion can follow immediately.
2. Meanings and possible misunderstandings can be clarified before continuing.
3. The teacher knows that every student has heard the story. As we all know, even if the book has been assigned as homework or as class reading, the assumption cannot be made, unfortunately, that it has been read by every student.

The disadvantages to reading books aloud include the following:

1. No matter how sensitively you pace your reading, each student requires a different length of time to think and discover or to look at the pictures.
2. The book is a physical barrier between you and your students. With that lessened contact comes lessened attention and involvement.
3. Students miss the feelings of mastery and control that come from having read the book themselves.

Even for students who cannot read at all, there are wonderful story books. Ann Jonas's (1983, 1985) books are excellent for all ages, including preschoolers. Mercer Mayer's (1967, 1968, 1969) frog books are delightful to "read," even though they have no words, as are Alexandra Day's (1990, 1991a, 1991b, 1992a, 1992b, 1993, 1994) books about Carl the Rottweiler. These are wonderful books for students to "read" by themselves in a quiet corner.

Chris Van Allsburg's (1984) *The Mysteries of Harris Burdick* is for older students. This is a book of wonderfully crafted pictures, each accompanied by one evocative sentence. The class can speculate as a group what story would follow, or your students can work individually and then share. It will be fun to see how many different stories each picture can generate. There are two directories of picture books with few or no words (Lima & Lima, 1989; Wilson & Moss, 1988).

Plays

A classroom unit on a classic or contemporary play has merit in and of itself. Plays can be read aloud in class or assigned to be read as homework. Students can be assigned a character's part to read in a reader's theater type of presentation, in which lines do not have to be learned. Plays also can be performed in part or entirely in as simple or elaborate a production as desired. Students can write their own plays for performance, either about units being studied or about their own lives. This can be done collaboratively or alone. Many of the story games in this book involve playwriting, and many more of the activities suggest dramatization as a variation and/or follow-up.

Poetry

Poetry gives melody and imagery to the written word and adds rhythm and flow when spoken aloud. Rhymes help us to remember songs and poems, which in turn help us to remember all sorts of things, from Mother Goose stories and finger plays to some very specialized information. For example, anatomy students remember the names of the 12 cranial nerves by this little mnemonic poem, in which the first letter of each word is the first letter of each nerve, in order: "On old Olympus' towering top, a Finn and German viewed a hop."

Poetry adds enrichment and can be an essential part of the story. Can you imagine "Hansel and Gretel" without "Nibble, nibble, little mouse, who's that nibbling at my house?" or "Jack and the Beanstalk" without the "Fee, Fi, Fo, Fum . . . ?"

A poem also can be the form in which a story is told, as in Longfellow's (1900/1983) *Hiawatha* or *Beowulf* (1000/1992). Songs are poems set to music, from folk ballads such as *Barbara Allen* to popular jingles such as *How Much Is That Doggie in the Window?* Rap music is as much poetry as it is music. Students can learn the poems used in stories and chant them at appropriate times during the telling. This makes them participants in the telling and keeps their interest.

In summation, classic books, plays, and poetry should be read aloud to teach appreciation for beautiful words and imagery and also to introduce a unit on creative writing or poetry. Books, plays, and poetry can themselves be story starters for many of the activities in this book. Some examples of literature-related activities follow.

Literary Arts Activities

Retelling. Ask your students to retell the story of a book, play, or poem in their own words.

Alternative Endings. Discuss possible alternative endings to a story read in class or assigned. Discuss what might have happened after the story ended. If they lived happily ever after, how did they do that? Ask your students to write a different ending to the story.

Update. Update the time and place of a story the class has been studying and discuss how the story would change. A prince might become a senator, knights might become Green Berets, a magician might become a healer or a scientist, or a princess might become a rock star. This is a very popular device for storytellers. For example, in the movie *Cinderfella,* the mistreated stepchild is a teenage boy. Shakespeare's plays have been done in every setting imaginable. For example, *West Side Story* is a retelling of *Romeo and Juliet* set in modern New York City, and *Forbidden Planet* is a retelling of *The Tempest* in a science fiction setting. Ask your students to write an updated version of a story they have read.

Translated Literature. Read translated literature from another culture aloud or show a foreign film with subtitles and discuss similarities and differences between cultures. Ask your students to take an incident from the story and rewrite it as it might happen to a person living in this time and place.

Act It Out. Have your students dramatize parts of the book, play, or poem they have been studying. They can take the parts of the characters, using the words provided by the text, to make the story come alive for them. Or they can improvise dialogue for their assigned characters based on facts and suggestions given by the text. They can go on to improvise incidents and action suggested or implied by the text and can continue the story line beyond the ending provided by the original author.

Write a Poem. Ask your students to write a poem about the plot or characters of the book they are studying. This poem need not stick to the original story but could be about how they feel after hearing or reading the book, play, or poem.

Comparisons. Ask your students to gather pictures and descriptions from the time period described in the book they are studying. Discuss what the people wore, how they traveled, how the interiors and exteriors of their buildings looked, and how that time period compares with the present. Ask your students to use that information to imagine themselves living in that time and place and to write a story about it.

Time Line. Ask your students to make a time line of the period of the book being studied, showing what was happening in the world at that time and what events would have affected the characters. This can be done as a group class project or individually. Discuss how world events affect individuals. Ask your students to write a story about how a world event affected them and their families.

Rap. Ask your students to retell or create a story using rap rhythms, either throughout the story or in selected places.

TABLE 3.1 Grade-Level Guidelines: Literary Arts

	K-12	PK-2	3-5	6-12
Retelling	X			
Alternative Endings	X			
Update			X	X
Translated Literature			X	X
Act It Out	X			
Write a Poem			X	X
Comparisons			X	X
Time Line			X	X
Rap			X	X
Headlines			X	X

Headlines. Cut the headlines from newspaper stories, especially from the tabloids. Save the stories separately from the headlines. Ask your students to choose a headline and write a story to go with it. Can you imagine the stories you might get from these headlines?

> Fountain of Youth Discovered in Land Fill
> Space Aliens Held Me Captive for Two Weeks
> Mermaid Found in Tuna Trawler's Nets
> Forced to Become a Wolfman When the Moon Is Full
> Authentic Treasure Map Found in Attic
> Bigfoot Seen in Shopping Mall

The entire class can write about the same headline, or each student can be given a different headline to write about. When the stories are written, share and compare them with one another and then with the original story that you have saved separately.

Literary forms can be combined in a story. The following story was told with a fourth-grade class. It incorporates riddles, jokes, and a jump rope jingle, all of which were contributed by the students. Each student also learned to say his or her name backwards for the story. Their teacher had been reading *Through the Looking Glass* to them, and the class discussed what life would be like if everyone were part of a chess game. I used the class as characters in the story.

I provided some of the structure and asked for input as the story developed. As much as possible, I incorporated student ideas into the story as I told it. For example, in the second paragraph of the story below, I furnished, "Life was very hard for pawns in the second square. They worked from dawn until late at night. What sort of jobs did they do?" The students suggested chores, some of which became part of the story.

Throughout the storytelling, the students contributed many plot points and descriptions. The entire interactive storytelling technique is explained in detail in Group Storybuilding (see p. 61).

The interactive telling of this story took about 12 minutes. Later, I wrote down what I could remember of the story. I did not tape-record the collaborative effort, although that is certainly something you could do.

In this story, I have italicized those ideas contributed by the students.

Story: Looking-Glass Land

This is a story about a time when life was like a chess game. All of the fourth graders started out as pawns in their home square. If they could cross six borders, they would enter the eighth square and become kings or queens, just as Alice did when she went through the Looking Glass.

Life was very hard for pawns in the second square. They worked from dawn until late at night, *cleaning, polishing, sewing, digging, scrubbing, and cooking.* One midnight after the work was done, all the pawns met at the stables and made plans to run away to the eighth square. Each one had *a knapsack filled with food from the kitchen and a leather flask of water.*

They traveled only after dark and slept in trees during the day. Finally, they crossed the border to the third square and were able to travel by day. They walked all day and when it got dark, they saw a *cabin with light shining out of the windows.*

The children were so glad to see the place. They knocked on the door and asked for food and shelter. What they didn't know was that this was a bandits' lair. The bandits invited the children in and gave them food and milk to drink. In the milk was a *sleeping potion. The bandits planned to sell the children as slaves.*

When the children fell asleep, the bandits *put them into sacks and threw them in the back of a wagon and drove off to meet the slavers.* The thumping and bumping of the wagon woke the children. They *cut themselves free and jumped off the wagon,* which rolled along without them. Luckily the wagon had carried them across the border to the fourth square.

In this square, everyone *jumped rope all the time,* even while they were eating. The children crossed this square without any trouble because they were all good jump ropers. In order to cross the border, however, they had to say a jump rope rhyme. So all together they said, *"Cinderella, dressed in yellow, went upstairs to kiss a fellow. Made a mistake and kissed a snake. How many doctors will it take? One, two, three . . ."* and before they got to 10, they were in the fifth square.

In this square, everyone *rode bicycles,* which was easy, so the children rode right into the sixth square, which was a place where *everything was backward.* Everyone said *"Good-bye" instead of "Hello"* and said *"Yes" when they meant "No."* They laughed *when they were sad and cried when they were happy.* It took a little getting used to, but the children were able to get to the border. All they had to do to cross into the seventh square was to say their names backward. [Each student said his or her name backward.]

The seventh square was the *land of riddles.* Everyone talked in riddles and never got any work done. In order to cross the last border, each child had to tell a riddle to be added to the riddle treasury. These are the riddles they told:

Q. Why did the radish kiss the banana?
A. Because it had a-peel.
Q. What's the best way to catch a squirrel?
A. Climb a tree and act like a nut.
Q. What has four legs, a tail, and a trunk?
A. A mouse going on vacation.
Q. Why did the chicken cross the road?
A. To get to the other side.
Q. What goes up and never comes down?
A. Your age.
Q. What's green and white, has four legs, and hops?
A. A frog sandwich.

Q. Where's the biggest diamond in the world?
A. In Yankee Stadium.
Q. What are you when you get out of school?
A. Old.
Q. Why did the duck cross the road?
A. To get to the other side.
Q. Why did the pickle sneeze?
A. Because he was allergic to flowers.
Q. What has big ears and a big trunk and weighs only four
    ounces?
A. A mouse going on a trip.
Q. How did the elephant get to school?
A. By bus.
Q. What goes down and never up?
A. Rain.

The children crossed over into the eighth square, and they all
got to be kings and queens, and they lived happily ever after.

The End

Visual Arts

Whether used as inspiration or illustration, artwork supplies a stimulating and enriching addition to storytelling. All kinds of art can be used,
such as classic paintings, pictures from publications, posters, cartoons,
collages, student drawings and paintings, sculpture, baskets, prehistoric
artifacts, puppets, toys, and other objects.

After a story has been read or created, students can draw or paint
pictures of their favorite part. They can work cooperatively on a large
mural or collage or make smaller individual ones. They can draw cartoons
or color line drawings supplied to them. A story quilt can be sewn. In fact,
students can work in clay, flannel or other fabrics, wood, glass, or any
other material and technique that can be thought of. Peeker bottles can be
made out of discarded plastic bleach bottles, where a peek through the
small opening will reveal a scene from a story.

Art is used when a story is dramatized. Even when no costumes or
scenery are used, students will want to make simple props, such as a magic
wand or a crown. More elaborate productions will use costumes, scenery,
furniture, and props, which can all result from art projects.

Finger puppets, hand puppets, rod puppets, or marionettes can be used to dramatize a story, as can stuffed animals. When using a puppet, be sure to keep it in motion, if only to nod its head or to move its body for emphasis. Otherwise, the illusion that the puppet is alive is broken.

A fascinating combination of visual art and storytelling occurs when the storyteller makes a line drawing on the board with chalk or with markers on a large pad of paper while telling the story. The picture and the story are finished at the same time. This technique really holds the attention of everyone in the audience. A similar combination of art forms occurs when the storyteller cuts or tears folded paper while telling the story. At the end of the story, the paper is unfolded to reveal an object relevant to the story, such as a tree or a line of men attached at the hands.

I, myself, cannot draw, shred, or cut, and people who can have my admiration, even though I feel inadequate when I watch them. The fact that they smile and tell me how easy it is doesn't help me at all. Among the best practitioners of these techniques that I personally know are school librarians. I have seen books and articles about these techniques, so if you are interested in trying your hand at these craft-y methods, I'll bet your school librarian could help you.

In summation, art can be used to inspire, illustrate, and enrich a story or can result from the inspiration and ideas that a story gives. Some examples of art-related activities follow.

Visual Arts Activities

Picture Sequencing. After a story has been told or read in class, ask your students to draw or paint a picture of their favorite part of the story. Arrange all the pictures in sequence. The student who painted each picture will tell his or her part of the story. This activity teaches sequencing and trains memory.

Comic Strip. After a story has been told or read in class, ask your students to draw the sequence of the story in comic strip form. This is a good way to introduce the skill of outlining a story.

Story Map. Read a story in class. Ask your students to draw a story map to show where the events of the story happened and then to use the map to retell the story.

TABLE 3.2 Grade-Level Guidelines: Visual Arts

	K-12	PK-2	3-5	6-12
Picture Sequencing		X	X	
Comic Strip			X	
Story Map			X	
Flannel Board			X	
Random Pictures	X			
Prequels	X			
Art Objects	X			
Story Trade	X			
What Is It?			X	X

Flannel Board. Read or tell a story in class. Have your students make flannel figures and use them to retell the story on a flannel board. Alternatively, have them make flannel figures for a story of their own choosing and tell it to the class using a flannel board.

Random Pictures. Cut out interesting pictures from magazines and place them in individual envelopes. Have your students choose an envelope, show the picture to their classmates, and make up a story about it.

Prequels. Show a picture to the class and speculate with them about the people in it. (What are they like? What are they doing in the picture? What could have been the events that led up to whatever they are doing?) Ask your students to write or tell a story about the events that led up to the picture being discussed. You also might ask them to speculate about what will happen next.

Art Objects. Bring art objects and artifacts from another culture to class. Speculate with your students about what kind of a society would produce this kind of work. Ask your students to make up a story about the objects being used by someone from that culture and time.

Story Trade. Ask your students to select a picture or art object that has been brought into class. Have them choose partners and take turns telling their partners a story about the chosen object. Then have them switch objects and make up two different stories.

What Is It? Ask your students to assemble an object from various materials such as wood, fabric, rubber, plastic, and so on and bring it to class. This object should have no known purpose. Speculate about the possible uses of the items they have assembled. Ask them to write a story about their object, or you may prefer that your students exchange objects with one another and create stories about the other object.

In summation, art can be incorporated into most of the activities in this book, and many examples are given throughout. The following story was inspired by some construction paper windsocks made as an art project by third-grade students. They were delighted to have their art project figure so prominently in the story. They did the chant, with its gestures, and enthusiastically howled like the wind.

Story: Windsocks

One day, the third-grade class made beautiful windsocks in class. They took them outside to test them. While they were trying to catch the wind with their windsocks, a cyclone came out of nowhere and carried off the windsocks with the children holding on to them. (Wind noises.)

They blew over mountains and an ocean and finally the wind slowed and gently set them down on the ground. It was good to be safe on the ground, but safe on the ground . . . where? Some of the children were worried that they'd miss supper, but mostly they worried about what to do next.

They decided to split up into two groups and explore in opposite directions. They hid all the windsocks in a cave except for two of them. Each group kept one in order to signal to the other, in case they found anything.

The first group turned right and followed a path. Soon they came to a small village. The children decided to hide behind some boulders and watch for a while before they went into the village to see whether it was safe. It's lucky that they did, because almost immediately they saw the other group of children being herded at spearpoint by a hunting party from the village. They had been captured! The hidden children watched their classmates being put into a cage.

The natives built a fire and put a huge pot of water over the fire to heat. They were going to cook the children! The natives kept chanting

"Higgery, diggery" (Pair off. Alternately clap hands together and then clap partner's hands.)

"Yum, yum, yum" (Rub stomachs in circular motion with one hand.)

"Hoggery, doggery" (Alternately clap hands together and then clap partner's hands.)

"Yum!" (Rub stomach with both hands.)

(Repeat three times.)

When the water was hot, the natives went to get the children out of the cage, and as they did, the natives saw the signal windsock. The natives had never seen such a thing and were fascinated by it. They kept pointing to it and making noises of wonder. That gave the hidden group an idea.

They ran back to the cave to get the rest of the windsocks, which they brought into the village. The natives were still chanting. (Repeat chant.) By using signs, the children made the natives understand that they could have all the windsocks if they let the captured children go free. The natives decided they would rather have the windsocks than child stew and let the children go.

Everyone walked away from the village as fast as possible. The children could hear the natives chanting as they walked. (Repeat chant.) The sound got fainter and fainter until they left the natives far behind. (Gradually decrease volume of the chanting until it can't be heard.)

Then the children started to think of ways to get back home. [The students made many suggestions and then voted to determine which method of return to use in the story.] They decided to build a raft. They gathered large leaves to use as sails to catch the wind. Before they could fasten them, another cyclone came and blew all the children back home while they held tightly to their big leaves. (Wind noises.)

They made some more windsocks and hung them in the classroom, and if no one has moved them, they're hanging there still.
The End

Musical Arts

Music can be an integral part of a story, as in opera, or can give a
story or play new form. *South Pacific* is a resetting of Michener's *Tales
of the South Pacific,* and *West Side Story* is an updating of *Romeo and
Juliet.* Musicals can also use a composer's music as inspiration for a story.
Song of Norway uses Grieg's melodies, as *Kismet* uses those of Borodin.

In the foregoing examples, music is a necessary part of the story. In
other plays and in many films, music adds to the enjoyment but is not
essential to the plot. In all the Fred Astaire-Ginger Rogers films, the songs
(and dances) could be removed and the story would remain, but what a
loss that would be! The same holds true for almost any film or play done
before 1940. *Oklahoma* was the first Broadway play to use song and dance
as essential parts of the plot by having them further the story instead of
being mere musical insertions.

During plays and films, music is used as background to establish
moods, build suspense, startle, soothe, and excite. Sometimes, certain
characters or situations have their own melodies or *leitmotifs* (see Glossary). Music signals the beginning and end of the story, as well as inter-
missions. Used at the beginning, music prepares the viewer to enter a state
in which he or she suspends disbelief and sets the desired mood. Used at
the end, it provides closure and readies the viewer for return to the every-
day world.

Many musical works have been inspired by stories, such as Rimsky-
Korsakov's *Scheherazade* or Copland's *Billy the Kid.* Some music has been
written to accompany a specific spoken story, such as Prokofiev's *Peter
and the Wolf,* or sometimes the music comes first, as in Disney's *Fanta-
sia.* As previously stated, song is itself a story in poem form that has been
set to music.

Music can be a valuable part of storytelling. The storyteller can sing
or play an instrument as part of the performance. Songs can be taught to
the audience to sing as part of the story.

TABLE 3.3 Grade-Level Guidelines: Musical Arts

	K-12	*PK-2*	*3-5*	*6-12*
Pictures	X			
Daydreams			X	X
Feelings			X	X
Popular Songs			X	X
Biographies				X
Character Descriptions				X
Background			X	X
Leitmotifs			X	X
Folk Songs	X			
Opera				X
Sound Effects		X	X	
Music Makers		X		

Musical Arts Activities

Pictures. As they listen to music, have your students draw or paint a picture. Have them share the pictures and then use them to create a story, either collaboratively or individually.

Daydreams. While they listen to music, ask your students to write down any words that occur to them. Tell them not to worry about making sense or sentences. When the music is over, ask them to review what they have written and to think about it. Discourage them from talking to anyone during this time. Then ask them to write a poem or a story based on what they have written.

Feelings. After they have listened to music, have your students write a poem about the music and about how it made them feel. Give them a choice as to whether to use free verse, special forms, and/or rhyme.

Popular Songs. Ask your students to write a story about a familiar or popular song. They can either write the story that the song tells, tell a story about how it might have come to be written, or make up a story in which one or more of the characters sings the song as part of the action in the story.

Biographies. Ask your students to write a story about the life of a composer as they think it might have been, from listening to his or her music, and then compare it with an actual biography or autobiography.

Character Descriptions. Ask your students to do a character description of a composer, as they think he or she might have been, from listening to the composer's music. They can use the Character Description Forms (see Resources) if desired. Have them compare with information contained in an actual biography.

Background. Ask your students to find suitable music for a chosen or assigned story and to tell the story to the class, using the music they have found as background. Music students can write original music and either record it for their own storytelling or accompany another student storyteller.

Leitmotifs. Explain the use of leitmotifs to your class (see Glossary). Have your students tell a story to the class using a different musical theme for each character and situation. Unless they can accompany themselves on an instrument, the students probably will need an assistant to operate the sound equipment.

Folk Songs. Ask each student to learn a folk song from another culture and teach it to the class. If every student does this, the class will learn a lot of songs. A program of these songs could be recorded or presented as a concert.

Opera. Have your class improvise an "opera" by having several students "sing" a story they already know. Advanced students can create an original story while they are "singing" it. This sounds much more difficult than it is, and students usually enjoy this activity very much.

Sound Effects. Have your students add sound effects to a story wherever appropriate. Creaking doors, gusts of wind, eerie sounds, and animal noises can be made vocally. They can devise ways to make other sounds, such as doors slamming, footsteps, hoof beats, scratching, and so on. "The Bremen Town Musicians" is fun to do in this manner.

Music Makers. Distribute musical instruments, such as bells, drums, kazoos, tambourines, and cymbals. Ask your students to make up a story using these instruments. Each student can be a musician in the story. This is an excellent activity for physically challenged students. They can make "music" at appropriate times while the teacher tells the story. In one of my classes, there was a girl with cerebral palsy whose voluntary movement was limited to nodding her head slightly. Another student was appointed as her assistant, whose job it was to bang the cymbals whenever she nodded her head.

Movement Arts

Much of what we have said about music applies to dance. In classical ballet, dancers tell the story without spoken words. In musical plays, dance is often an essential part of the story, as in the fight scenes in *West Side Story* or the scene in *Lili* in which the main character realizes she loves the puppeteer.

Dance and dancers can inspire stories, such as *A Chorus Line* and *Tap*. And stories can be written about famous dancers, such as *All That Jazz* and *Nijinsky*. Even when it is not essential to the plot, dance makes an important contribution. Can you imagine *Singing in the Rain* without the dance numbers? None of them are essential to the plot, but their loss would be sorely felt. As a group activity, ask your students to watch a musical play or film. Discuss whether the dancing was necessary to the plot. (What did the dancing add to the story? Would it have been as entertaining without the dancing?)

Pantomime is a type of stage movement without sound. In pantomime, movements are natural and realistic as opposed to the stylized, exaggerated movements of the mime. Special training is required to be a mime, but careful observation is all that is necessary to be able to pantomime accurately.

Pantomime is an excellent technique to use when you are beginning to dramatize stories. Much of acting is done with gesture and facial expression, and pantomime focuses on those essentials without the distraction of trying to think of what to say. To help your students appreciate the physical aspects of acting, ask them to watch a television sitcom (not one with a puppet) with the sound turned off. Talk about how much they were able to understand without words to help them.

Another benefit of pantomime is that it can be done as a group. Ordinarily, self-conscious students have no difficulty pantomiming in unison with the rest of their class because there is no separate focus on them.

Another type of gesture is rhythmic movement, such as the finger snapping and the body movements of "rappers." Hand clapping and arm gestures, often accompanied by finger snapping, are used for counting games and to punctuate songs and chanting games. Many preschool, camp, and kindergarten songs have movements to accompany certain words, such as *The Eensy Weensy Spider* and *The Five Little Ducks.* Let's go even younger—babies love to play *Peek-a-Boo.*

Movement and gesture are part of every story to some degree, including the movements we make unconsciously when we are talking. Body language and facial expression, as well as gesture and movement, are part of the characterization and description that enrich and amplify stories (see Chapter 5). The following movement-related activities will help your students to become more aware of the importance of including such descriptions in their stories and will give them practice in doing so.

Movement Arts Activities

Ballet. Ask your students to attend a ballet or to watch it on television. Ask them to tell or write the story of the ballet in their own words and share it with the class.

Biography. Ask your students to read a biography of a famous dancer and share their book reports with the class before handing them in.

Mime. Have your class watch a mime perform, either in person or on videotape. Ask your students to write or tell the story that they inferred by watching and compare the different interpretations in class.

Folk Dance. Teach your students a folk dance from a different culture. Discuss what the dance movements seem to symbolize and then ask them to write a story about what you have discussed or about the people from that culture who would be the dancers.

Act It Out. I got the idea for this activity and the next one from Viola Spolin (1963). Instruct your students to let their bodies show different emotions such as fear, joy, confusion, sorrow, or anger. If you make this a unison activity with everyone working at the same time, you will get less self-consciousness from your students. Ask your students to write a paragraph describing the appearance and behavior of a character who is feeling one of these emotions.

TABLE 3.4 Grade-Level Guidelines: Movement Arts

	K-12	PK-2	3-5	6-12
Ballet			X	X
Biography			X	X
Mime	X			
Folk Dance		X	X	
Act It Out	X			
What Is It?	X			
Moving	X			
Charades			X	X

What Is It? Instruct your students to pantomime holding and carrying objects of different weights, such as a balloon, a pillow, a pail of water, or a large boulder. Write the names of such objects on slips of paper, which will be drawn at random by the students. Students will pantomime holding or carrying the object they have drawn. The class will try to guess what item is being carried. Discuss what worked and what would have been more helpful to show. Repeat until everyone has had a turn. Ask your students to write a paragraph describing the physical appearance and behavior of a character carrying an object up a hill—for example, a heavy suitcase.

Moving. Have everyone walk in a circle around the room. While the students are moving, suggest various ways for them to walk—for example, walking as if you had just been given a million dollars. Move as if you've been working all day and are very, very tired. Walk as if you are 75 years old. Walk as if you are 3 years old. Ask your students to write a description of someone walking, without giving any information except physical description. See how much the class can tell about the character by hearing the physical description read to them.

Charades. Teach your class how to play charades. Form teams and play. You could have charades tournaments and could play other classes in competition.

Sign Language

Sign language is a language of gesture as well as an alternative to speech. Hearing students can benefit from learning sign language. It gives them another modality for learning and memory and also gives them another language to use. Of the three modalities of learning—visual, auditory, and kinesthetic—the last is the most often neglected. Sign language uses that kinesthetic approach.

When sign language is used, the improved communication between hearing and hearing-impaired students benefits everyone. Besides, it gives them a "secret" language that helps them to feel special and builds self-confidence. It also trains your students to look at you when you are talking.

A good way to introduce a unit on sign language is to invite hearing-impaired persons to visit your class to talk about themselves and their experiences. If there are hearing-impaired students in your class, they might be willing to share some of their experiences with their classmates. You might want to prepare your students ahead of time, so they can think about any questions they would like to ask. A good way to give your students an idea of what it is like to be hearing-impaired is to ask them to watch television with the sound turned off.

When teaching sign language, why not start with a few signs that might be useful for *you,* such as the signs for *wait, think,* or *take out your papers.* A good beginning activity is to teach your students a simple song with accompanying signs. Your students can practice using sign language with one another, gradually enlarging their vocabularies until they can tell a story in sign language while speaking simultaneously. Not everyone will gain the same proficiency, of course, but they will all gain a degree of new language skill. As they learn sign language, encourage your students to watch news broadcasts that use sign language interpreters alongside the newscaster and to go to plays that use sign language interpreters onstage.

You don't have to be proficient in using sign language before you can begin a unit on it in your classroom. Your learning specialist or librarian should be able to lend you a book about it. You can learn along with your students. As a matter of fact, if they have to help you to learn the signs or to remember them, what a boost to their self-worth that would be! And how wonderful for them to see you as a human being who, like them, sometimes forgets. I myself know very little sign language.

I have a story/song that I teach to preschoolers who have no difficulty with it at all. The children love it and request it often. It uses very few signs. First I teach the signs for *girl, boy,* and *where are you?* as well as the signs for *A* and *L.* When the sign for *girl* is made (touch thumb to side of chin) with the fingers in the *A* position (clenched fist), that signifies

Anne, and the sign for *boy* (touch temple with thumb) with the fingers in the *L* position (forefinger and thumb extended) signifies *Lou.*

Then I tell a simple repetitive story about Anne and Lou. Each time Lou or Anne's name is mentioned in the story, the children make the appropriate sign. Anne and Lou are siblings.

Story: Anne and Lou

Lou awakens early and goes into Anne's bedroom to surprise her. He yells "Boo!" (so does the class), but Anne isn't there. The children decide which room Lou goes to next to try to scare Anne. Lou yells "Boo!" again (along with the class), but again Anne isn't there. This is repeated a few more times, each time in a different room chosen by the class. Finally Lou returns to his bedroom, only to be scared by Anne (and the class) yelling "Boo!"

Then we sing the following song, to the tune of *Frere Jacques,* making the appropriate signs while we sing

Anne and Lou, Anne and Lou,

Where are you? Where are you? (Waggle forefinger back and forth, then point forward.)

Hiding in the bedroom, hiding in the bedroom. (Hide head behind arms.)

Peek-a-boo! Peek-a-boo! (Put hands in front of face and open for peek-a-boo.)

This verse is repeated, substituting a different room for "bedroom" until all the rooms the children suggested during the story have been used.

4

Working With Story Lines

Activities that teach the development of a story line should be introduced early because they teach the foundation on which all stories and plays are based—plot development. They also teach memory and sequencing.

Every plot has three basic parts:

1. Beginning: This is the section that introduces three subparts: characters, setting, and purpose. This purpose can be either a quest or a beginning action. Viola Spolin (1963) refers to these subparts as "Who," "Where," and "What."

2. Middle: This section contains the conflicts that carry the plot forward. These conflicts can be problems, moral issues, complications, obstructions, tests, or any other plot device that prevents the characters from reaching their goal. There may be a series of problems; as soon as one has been overcome, another presents itself, as in most adventure stories. Without conflict, there is no story. You might have a description or a tone poem, but not a story. Teachers tell me that this concept is the most difficult aspect of story writing to teach. The activities in this chapter are designed specifically to do this job. When facilitating group storybuilding in the classroom, it helps to remember that conflict propels the story forward. Whenever attention starts to wander or energy lessens, it's time to introduce another problem.

  3. *End:* In this section, all problems are solved, conflicts resolved, and tests completed; the goal is reached. Often, the characters undergo some changes and realizations in the resolution. Not all stories have happy endings. Only you can decide when unhappy endings are appropriate for your class, according to their maturity and experience. Unhappy endings motivate discussion and follow-up work. Sometimes, the resolution is withheld deliberately, as in Storybuilding 1-2 (see p. 64). An unfinished story keeps interest high as students try to achieve closure. We all want to know what happened next and how it ended.

  A good way to introduce the story line concept to your class is to read or tell them a story and then ask them as a group to identify the three main parts, especially the conflict (or conflicts, as stories become more complex). You can discuss the plots of movies or television shows they have seen, asking them to identify the conflicts in them and to see how crucial the conflicts are to the story.

  In previous sections of this book, I have offered several suggestions for activities that lead to student-generated stories. You probably will have to remind your class each time to be sure to make a problem or problems for their characters to solve in their stories.

  Telling a circle story is a good way to identify conflict. In the type of tale known as a circle story, the story ends where it began, and the conflicts repeat in each part of the story. "The Fisherman and His Wife" and "Hans in Luck" are two well-known examples. In the first, a poor fisherman catches a magic fish and sets it free. Pressed by his wife, the fisherman keeps asking the fish for gifts, each one greater than the last. Finally, the wife demands to rule the universe, and the fish returns her and her husband to their original poverty in retribution for their arrogance.

  In the second story, which has been told in different versions in many cultures, Hans has nothing, so he hires himself out for 7 years and receives a large piece of gold when he completes the 7 years. The gold is very heavy, so he trades it for a horse. He keeps making trades because everything is too heavy or too much trouble. Finally, he winds up with a grindstone that accidentally falls down a well, leaving him the way he started—penniless. He congratulates himself for getting rid of his burden.

This type of story may be a good way to introduce the concept of irony to your class and can spark a great deal of discussion.

Circle Story

Time estimate: 10 to 30 minutes. The last 20 minutes can be assigned as homework.
Suggested grade level: K through 12
Level of difficulty: Intermediate
Preparation: None

Comments

This type of story teaches sequencing and gives students an experience of following an assigned structure in their writing. The story that follows this activity was told by a first-grade girl and written down by her teacher.

Procedure

1. Read a circle story to the class.
2. Discuss the story and its circular plotline.
3. Ask the students to write circle stories. This can be assigned as homework. Alternatively, the class can collaborate in a group storytelling.
4. Have students share their stories, either by telling or reading to the class. A book can be made of these stories.

Variations

- Use the blackboard to plot the story line on a circular story map, beginning and ending in the same space.
- Have your students illustrate the story by drawing or painting episodes of the story in a circular format.
- Have your students dramatize the story, with or without costumes, sets, and props.

Story: The Flea

Once there was a flea. He was happy. One day a cat scratched him and tried to bite him. The flea said, "It is better to be a cat." Poof! He was a cat. He liked it. He chased mice. One day he was chased by a dog. He said, "It is better to be a dog." Poof! He was a dog. He was happy. Then a flea bit him. He said, "It is better to be a flea." Poof! He was a flea. He was happy. He stayed a flea.
The End

Unfinished Story

Time estimate: 10 to 30 minutes. The last 20 minutes can be assigned as homework.
Suggested grade level: K through 12
Level of difficulty: Beginning/intermediate
Preparation: None

Comments

This activity uses the concept of basic story line parts. It furnishes characters, settings, purpose, and conflict to the students and allows them to supply the ending of the story.

Procedure

1. Begin to read or tell a story to the class.
2. Stop the story before the resolution of the main problem. For example, this could be a story about a boy who has lost his bicycle, which he needs to deliver newspapers.
3. Restate the problem that needs to be solved.
4. Ask the students to volunteer some possible solutions. Spend 2 to 3 minutes on this.
5. Ask your students to write their own individual endings to the story.
6. Share the different endings in class.

Variation

⊗ A book can be made that begins with the story as told in class, followed by all the collected endings.

Hints

⊗ The lower grades can dictate their endings, which can be written down for them.

⊗ Step 4 is very important. It provides suggestions for those students who have difficulty coming up with their own ideas and ensures a successful experience for them. Your more creative students will springboard from those ideas discussed in class.

Basic 1-2-3

Time estimate: 10 to 15 minutes
Suggested grade level: 1 through 3
Level of difficulty: Beginning
Preparation: None

Comments

This activity introduces the three basic parts to a story and is designed to help students identify the beginning, conflict, and resolution of a story. Some of the story line activities in this chapter use the term *1-2-3* after a theater improvisation game by that name that has been used by so many actors and directors that it is impossible to find out who was the originator. I first learned it as a repertory member of the Lady Bug Theater, a professional theater for children in Portland, Oregon.

The term 1-2-3 is used to emphasize the three basic parts of a story line. They are all that is necessary for a complete story. Description and characterization add dimension, but they are not essential.

Procedure

1. Review the three main parts to a story (see pp. 45-46).

2. Tell students you are going to read or tell a story to them, and they are to raise the appropriate number of fingers (one, two, or three) when they hear the corresponding part of the story.
3. Read or tell the story.
4. Review, discussing when each part occurred in the story.

Variation

▪ Have students suggest a well-known story. After making sure everyone in class knows the story, ask the class to identify the three basic parts. Proceed to another well-known story and repeat.

Hint

▪ Making this a group activity will provide peer models for those students who are slower to grasp the ideas without putting undue pressure on them to perform.

Mixed-Up Start-Up

Time estimate: 10 to 30 minutes. The last 20 minutes can be assigned as homework.
Suggested grade level: 3 through 12
Level of difficulty: Intermediate
Preparation: None

Comments

This activity is excellent for helping students to gain mastery over the basics of story construction. It should not be used until students are familiar with the 1-2-3 concept.

Procedure

1. Review the three main parts of a story (see pp. 45-46). Tell your students they are going to make up a story, starting with the middle of the story or problem.

2. Have your students select a problem to tell a story about—for example, a group of people who are lost in a swamp.
3. Generate questions with the class such as, Who is lost? Does anyone else know about it? How did it happen? Are there any dangers? Were they looking for something or someone? Do they get rescued? How? Write all questions on the board.
4. Have students write their own individual stories, using their own answers to the questions written on the board.
5. Have students share their stories, either by telling or reading them to the class.

Variations

- Proceed in the same manner, starting from the end of the story. The endings that work best with this type of story development are often morals, such as "Honesty is the best policy," or the type of story that tells how an animal got its characteristics. In these stories, the ending must already be known before the story can be created. You might introduce this activity by reading a story such as "How the Bear Lost His Tail" or one of Kipling's *Just So Stories.* Every culture has stories that tell how things came to be the way they are.
- Ask your students to write their own how and why stories or have your class collaborate on creating stories together. Here is a list of possible subjects:

  How the zebra got its stripes
  How the camel got its hump
  How the leopard got its spots
  How the elephant got its trunk
  Why oysters make pearls
  How the rhino got so baggy
  Why bats sleep upside down
  How the gorilla lost its tail
  Why the hyena laughs

These stories can be collected in a book to use as reading resources or can be shared with other classes.

The following is a how and why story written by a second-grade boy:

Story: Why Some Ducks Are Green

Once there was a flock of brown ducks. They didn't like being brown. They would rather be yellow or white because they thought brown was ugly.

They were headed north for the summer when they flew over a nuclear reactor that blew up. All of the air around them was radioactive.

They landed in a pond near the reactor. All of a sudden they started turning green. It started at the tip of their beaks and worked its way down.

Ever since then they have been very mad and very, very, very green.

The End

Round Robin

Time estimate: 10 to 15 minutes
Suggested grade level: K through 12
Level of difficulty: Beginning
Preparation: None

Comments

In this type of activity, students contribute consecutively to a story. Round robins are good for students who seldom volunteer in class. Everyone will have a turn and can prepare for it if he or she has trouble being spontaneous. No one can be overlooked, and the "eager beavers" can't monopolize the story. You don't have the distraction of children trying to get your attention by raising their hands or making noises. Because each student speaks in order going around the circle, being first or last is not an issue, especially if you vary where in the circle you start each time.

This is a great activity for teaching listening skills. If the students stop paying attention when it isn't their turn, switch to random order. That way, the students have to go on listening, because they never know when their turn will come.

Round robins as a group contain some of the easiest and some of the most difficult storytelling activities included in this book. They tend to be more rambling than stories told by other methods. When written down, they may require editing and additional details to ensure conflict and continuity, but the finished product is fresh and original, often with surprising plot twists.

Procedure

1. Have the students sit in a circle, either at desks or on the floor.
2. Tell your students that they are going to make up a story with each student contributing consecutively.
3. Choose a topic or starting sentence for the story. A sample starting sentence might be, "On my way to the store, I saw the most unusual thing!"
4. Have each student add to the story in turn, until all students have participated. The length of each contribution can be predetermined, or you can decide the time to switch to the next student.
5. Continue until everyone has had a turn, with the last speaker ending the story.
6. Have your students write the story they have just created, making any changes they like. Remind them that their written stories must have conflict and resolution.

The story that follows was developed by a sixth-grade class that used this activity. I think they did a good job of relating each idea to the previous one as the story passed from each student to the next, and they managed to tie the story up neatly.

Variations

- Speakers are not chosen by the teacher or by their place in the circle. The student speaking chooses the next speaker and the time to switch by pointing or tossing a bean bag. It is fun to switch in the middle of a sentence.
- The topic or starting sentences can relate to a unit being studied. For example, if the unit is on the Revolutionary War: "The men were grumbling about this latest tax on tea. They were gathered at Tina's house, and she could hear them in the other room."

- ※ The last speaker does not end the story. The activity is interrupted and the students finish the story for themselves, either at their desks or as homework. These individual stories are later shared.
- ※ Begin and end the story with the same sentence, making a circle story (see p. 47). The entire class will have to cooperate to get the story back to the first sentence.
- ※ Decide on a first sentence and a last sentence before the story is begun. The last to speak must use the last sentence to end the story, but the whole class will have to help develop the story toward its prechosen ending to avoid creating a story in which the ending comes out of nowhere.
- ※ Have students remain at their desks instead of sitting in a circle. The first student writes the beginning of a story on a piece of paper and then passes the paper to the next student. Each student adds to the story until all have had a turn and/or the story is completed. In this variation, each student can contribute a paragraph or more, as desired. The story can be written or typed, or it can be done on a computer, with each student taking a turn. Those students not engaged in writing on the paper can either do homework, an in-class assignment, or read a book. The completed story is read to the class, and each student can receive a copy.

Hint

- ※ If the students interrupt excessively or distract each other with physical contact, this activity is best done with them seated at their desks in a circle. Putting them behind wood and metal not only gives them physical separation but also encourages impulse control because it re-creates a more structured classroom situation.

Story: The Intergalactic Football Game

Smalltown was hosting the first intergalactic football game between Smalltown and Mars. The Martians were staying in the homes of Smalltown's sixth-grade children. Some of the Martians had strange habits, although they didn't seem strange to the Martians, of course.

For example, they shed their skins every night instead of bathing, and they curled up in a ball to sleep instead of lying down under the covers. Instead of snoring, they chanted "aum" and required the soft blue light of the television instead of sunshine. Strangest of all, they didn't eat Earth food. All they ate were little green slime balls that they brought with them in a sort of egg carton.

The day for the big game was approaching, but there was a problem. One of the Martians had fallen in love with the pet parrot that lived in the house where he was staying. He sat gazing at it all day instead of going to practice. He wrote love letters and love poems to the parrot. The Martian wanted to give the parrot a lovely present, so he fed it one of the green slime balls—and the parrot died.

The Martian was heartbroken and refused to play in the big game because he felt so bad. The people in Smalltown contributed to a fund and bought a new parrot and switched it with the dead one. The Martian felt much better but wouldn't go to play in the game unless he could take the parrot with him. So the parrot's cage was placed right next to the 50-yard line.

The game began, and it was a close one. In the fourth quarter, the score was 10 to 10, with Smalltown receiving. One of the spaceships hovering over the field to watch moved in closer. He got a little too close to the stands and the spectators panicked and started running around. In the confusion, the Martian kicker grabbed the parrot instead of the football and kicked it down the field. A Smalltown player caught it and ran all the way for a bird down. The referee wouldn't let it be counted.

Where was the football? The teams searched for it and found it inside the parrot cage. Another Martian had fallen in love with it and was gazing fondly at it. He refused to let it be kicked or thrown, so the game ended in a tie and the Martians went home.

The President sent a letter to the citizens of Smalltown thanking them for furthering intergalactic relations by being diplomatic enough to end the game with nobody losing it.

The End

Pocket Robin

Time estimate: 10 to 15 minutes
Suggested grade level: 2 through 12
Level of difficulty: Beginning/intermediate
Preparation: None

Comments

Like all round robin activities, this one teaches listening skills and stimulates imagination. It uses objects contributed by the students, although you may want to supplement the collection.

Procedure

1. Ask your students to contribute items from their pockets or desks, assuring them they will get them back. Explain that they are going to make up a round robin story (see Round Robin, p. 52) by using their collected articles.
2. Have your students sit in a circle, either at desks or on the floor.
3. Choose a topic or a starting sentence, or let the first article taken from the bag determine the beginning of the story.
4. Hand the bag of collected articles to the first speaker. Instruct the student to reach into the bag, select the first object he or she touches, and incorporate that article into the story.
5. Continue in this manner, passing the unused collection of articles to each speaker in turn, until all articles have been used or until everyone has had a turn and the story is ended.
6. Have your students write the story they have just created, making any changes they like. Remind them that their written stories must include conflict and resolution.

Surprise Robin

Time estimate: 10 to 15 minutes
Suggested grade level: 2 through 12
Level of difficulty: Beginning/intermediate

Preparation: Wrap a number of small objects, such as a whistle, a crayon, a plastic animal, and so on. Place the wrapped objects in a bag or box.

Comments

This round robin activity teaches spontaneity and listening skills. It stimulates creativity and adds the element of chance to the fun.

Procedure

1. Have your students sit in a circle, either at desks or on the floor.
2. Tell your students that they are going to make up a story with each student contributing consecutively (see Round Robin, p. 52). When their turn comes, they will take an object from the bag, unwrap it, and incorporate it into their part of the story.
3. Choose a topic or starting sentence for the story. Such a beginning might be, "The old mansion at the edge of town had been empty for years, but now, all of a sudden, there was a light in the upstairs window." If desired, let the first unwrapped object determine the beginning of the story.
4. Hand the bag of wrapped objects to the first speaker. Instruct him or her to reach into it and select an object, unwrap it, show it to the group, and then incorporate the object into the story. For example, if a student unwrapped a crayon, he or she might add, "I found a red crayon on the walk, and I know it wasn't there yesterday," or "A note dropped out of the window and fluttered to the ground. It was written with red crayon."
5. Pass the bag of wrapped objects to the next student, who will choose another object and incorporate it into the story.
6. Continue in this manner until each student has had a turn and the story is ended.
7. Have your students write the story they have just created, making any changes they like. Remind them that their written stories must include conflict and resolution.

Variations

▪ The wrapped items could be objects that represent a unit being studied, and the chosen topic could also relate to that unit.

* The last speaker does not end the story. After the story has gone around the circle, students finish the story for themselves, either at their desks or as homework.

Hints

* If the objects are put into small paper bags instead of being wrapped, the bags can be opened easily and later reused. Not only do you have less mess, but the students cannot identify the objects by feeling them before they are selected.
* Sometimes it is difficult for the last student in the circle to tie up all the loose ends and finish the story. In this case, let the entire class make suggestions as to how the story might be ended. Only very rarely will you have to do it for them.

Touchie-Feelie Robin

Time estimate: 10 to 15 minutes
Suggested grade level: 2 through 12
Level of difficulty: Intermediate
Preparation: Small unwrapped objects are placed in a drawstring bag or a "touchie-feelie" box. A simple one can be made by cutting a circle in one side of a covered cardboard box. The student reaches into the box through the hole and can feel the objects inside but cannot see them. Use items with different shapes and textures, such as a key, a small rubber ball, a bean bag, a feather, or a piece of sandpaper.

Comments

This round robin activity adds another sense modality to the creative process and develops kinesthetic recognition. A blindfold can be used if students are comfortable with that idea. If using a blindfold, do not assume that everyone is having fun just because the students are laughing. Discuss possible feelings about the blindfold before using it and excuse any student who shows the slightest anxiety about it during the discussion or after the game has started.

Procedure

1. Have the students sit in a circle, either at desks or on the floor.
2. Tell your students that they are going to make up a round robin story (see Round Robin, p. 52), incorporating objects into the story that they must identify only by touch.
3. Pass the bag or box of objects. In turn, students will reach into the container and select an object, which they will use to begin the story. Tell them not to take the object out of the container to look at until their turn is over. If the students are comfortable being blindfolded, the object can be removed from the container and shown to the rest of the class, but the blindfolded student won't be able to see it until his or her turn is over. This adds another element of fun.
4. Continue in this manner until everyone has had a turn and/or the story is ended.
5. Have your students write the story they have just created, making any changes they want. Remind them that their written stories have to include conflict and resolution.

Variations

* Continue the story around the circle until all objects in the container have been used. The student choosing the last object ends the story.
* A sock could be worn over the hand to make identification more difficult.

Mystery Robin

Time estimate: 15 to 30 minutes
Suggested grade level: 6 through 12
Level of difficulty: Advanced
Preparation: Small timer, name tags

Comments

This is a round robin game that actors and storytellers play when they want to drive each other crazy and have fun while they're doing it. It is definitely not for beginners. The players will create a mystery story with as many characters in the story as there are players. I recommend that this game be played with no more than 10 participants. The rest of the class can be the audience until the "murderer" is revealed. Then another group of 10 can be chosen to play the next round.

During the telling, as with most mystery stories, suspicion is cast on several characters, only to have them die later and eliminate themselves as suspects. No one will know who the murderer really is until the end of the story.

Procedure

1. Players sit in a circle on the floor.
2. Tell your students they are going to play an advanced round robin story game (see Round Robin, p. 52). Read steps 3 through 8 of this procedure to them and answer any questions to be sure they understand the rules of the game.
3. Each player chooses a character to be in the story and writes his or her character's name on a name tag, which is worn where everyone can see it.
4. The first player sets the timer for 1 minute and begins the mystery story, using the characters the class has chosen. The first student establishes the setting, which might be an old mansion on a stormy night with the phone lines down, and continues telling the story until the timer rings.
5. The timer is quickly passed to the next player, who immediately resets the timer for 2 minutes and repeats everything the first player has told, within reason. If the second player forgets anything from the first telling, his or her character must "die" and become the first victim in the story. The "victim" chooses the method of death and then acts it out, often to uncomplimentary remarks about his or her acting ability. Then that player is "out" and free to make remarks about the other players' storytelling and acting prowess. If, however, the second player successfully remembers the first part of the story, that student then adds his or her own continuation until the timer rings.
6. If the second player has "died," the third player sets the timer for 2 minutes again and proceeds, starting from the beginning, adding the murder, suicide, or accident of the second player, and then adding more to the story. If the second player has been successful

in repeating everything the first player has said (within reason), the third player sets the timer for 3 minutes and proceeds as above, telling everything that already has been told, plus an additional segment of the story.

7. Continue in this manner. Each time a player is successful in repeating everything that has been already told, 1 minute is added to the timer. Each time a player "dies," the timer stays at the previous time setting.

8. Continue until only one player is left. That remaining character is the murderer.

Variation

※ To lessen the difficulty, this game can be played without requiring that participants talk for a set length of time. Removing the timer will relieve a lot of pressure.

Group Storybuilding

Time estimate: 15 to 20 minutes
Suggested grade level: K through 12
Level of difficulty: Beginning/intermediate
Preparation: None

Comments

Many of the activities in this book use the technique of group storybuilding. The idea of facilitating a class in such a creative effort, without a "script" to follow, may be daunting at first. I urge you to try it. This activity will lead you step-by-step through uncharted territory.

Group storybuilding is one of the finest whole-language activities I know. Besides providing choice, ownership, and relevance, the stories can be retold, written, and read aloud. When students help to create a story, they remember it and want to share it. In fact, I have had parents jokingly ask me how to stop their children from telling it over and over. Even if their particular suggestions have not been used in the story told as a group activity, the students have heard their ideas repeated and accepted by their teacher and their peers, and they always have the option of using their own ideas later when they write or retell the story. In fact, they are encouraged to do so. This activity ties in beautifully with holidays and other special occasions and is a natural for special units being studied.

Procedure

1. Review the three main parts of a story (see pp. 45-46).
2. Write three headings on the blackboard: Beginning, Problem, and Solution.
3. Have your students choose the main characters, a setting, and a quest. Write them on the blackboard under the heading "Beginning." (In the story that follows, a kindergarten class wanted to be characters in their own story. In addition, they chose Mother Goose characters in Mother Goose Land. The quest was simply for the class to meet some of the Mother Goose characters.)
4. Ask for a volunteer or choose a student to begin the story by putting some of the characters in a setting and establishing what the quest is. The class can make suggestions, and you or the designated student can choose which suggestion to use.
5. Ask students for a plot complication or problem. You will get several. Write them on the blackboard under the heading "Problem." Either choose one or let the students vote for their preference. (Some of the suggestions in our example were the following: "Have someone be lost." "Have a dragon eat everyone up." "Everyone falls asleep." "They find a castle." The children voted to have someone be lost, and they chose Miss Muffet for that honor.)
6. Ask students for suggestions on how to solve the problem. Write them on the blackboard under the heading "Solution." Have your students vote on the solution preferred or choose for them if they can't decide. Sometimes, I choose the solution myself if a particular one catches my fancy, either because of the possibilities it presents or because it makes me laugh. (Who says I can't be arbitrary?) Often I will choose a suggested solution if it has been made by a student who rarely contributes, because I want to encourage further efforts from that student. (The students decided to look for clues. Bo Peep's lost sheep were followed by the children in the story until they came to a castle).
7. Continue in this manner, getting problems and solutions from the students until the quest is completed. If you have several problems

in the story, draw a line connecting each problem with its solution. (The next problem was how to get across the moat to the castle because the drawbridge was up. They solved this problem, only to be faced by another problem. When they found Miss Muffet in the castle and all story ends were neatly tied up, the story was over.)

8. Have students retell or write the story. They may use their own or any other ideas that were not chosen for the group story, if they wish. These stories can be illustrated and a book made of the original and its "second-generation" stories. Younger grades can draw or paint pictures, which can be used to illustrate the story.

Variation

▪ In your story, transport your entire class to a magical place. A magical setting helps to free imagination and allow more possibilities. One of the final problems will be how they will get back to the classroom, which is never the way they left it—that would be too easy!

Hints

▪ Keep the characters in one or two groups in the story, because it is difficult to manage more than two subplots in this type of story.
▪ Be sure to acknowledge every suggestion, except the inappropriate ones. Before choosing, remind the class that if their ideas weren't used, they can use them themselves when they retell or write the story.
▪ Try to avoid using established characters, such as Donald Duck or Ninja Turtles, because they can act only in limited, predictable ways.

In the following story, I supplied the first paragraph. The rest of the story was developed by the students in response to prompts such as "What did they do? What did they see? Then what happened?" Solutions to each problem were elicited, and the ones included in the story were selected by vote. I supplied the last paragraph, and each student told what his or her present would be.

Story: Mother Goose Land

Once upon a time the afternoon kindergarten class went on a field trip to Mother Goose Land. They saw Jack and Jill and Little Bo Peep talking to each other. They seemed worried. The kindergarten children went over to see what the problem was. Jill said, "We can't find Little Miss Muffet. There's no one sitting on her tuffet, and the spider hasn't seen her."

The children offered to go look for Miss Muffet. They walked along the road and saw some sheep running through the meadow. "Look!" yelled one of the girls, "I'll bet that's Bo Peep's lost sheep! Let's follow them."

So they did, and soon they came to a castle. There was a deep moat around the castle. The drawbridge was up, so they couldn't cross over the moat. They sat down to try to figure best how to get across. A big bird flew over them, and one of the children said, "Why don't we ask the bird to fly us over?"

But there was the problem of getting the bird to agree to take them. The children said, "Please," but the bird shook his head "No." They thought and thought, and one of them got a great idea. "We could make a birdseed cake to pay for the ride."

The children made a big birdseed cake, and the bird was happy to fly them across the moat. They went inside the castle, and there they saw Miss Muffet and Bo Peep sitting at a big table. Miss Muffet smiled when she saw them. "You're just in time for my birthday party," she said, "Come and sit down."

The children sat down. They told her how worried her friends were. She smiled, "I left a note in Jack and Jill's pail. They'll come as soon as they find it. I didn't want the spider to find out where I am and frighten everyone."

She sent one of the boys to let the drawbridge down. Soon all the Mother Goose people were there—except the spider. Everyone had a wonderful time.

When it was time to go home, the children promised to come back again for a visit. Miss Muffet told them that when they got home, they would all find their hearts' desire as a present from her. [The students took turns telling what their heart's desire would be.]

The End

Storybuilding 1-2

Time estimate: 15 to 30 minutes. The last half can be assigned as
   homework.
Suggested grade level: K through 12
Level of difficulty: Beginning/intermediate
Preparation: None

Comments

This activity is a natural sequence to Unfinished Story (see p. 48). It
requires more class participation than Unfinished Story and is excellent
for motivating continued interest and effort.

Procedure

1. Review the three main parts of a story (see pp. 45-46).
2. Write three headings on the blackboard: Beginning, Problem, and
   Solution.
3. Have your students choose the main characters, a setting, and a
   quest. Write them on the blackboard under the heading "Beginning." (A first-grade class chose a prince, a princess, and a toad.
   They wanted the toad to be a king who was under a magic spell.
   The setting was an estate with a castle and a swamp. The quest,
   or purpose, was to break the magic spell.)
4. Ask for a volunteer or select a student to begin the story. Suggestions can be taken from the class for a beginning.
5. Have students suggest ideas for complicating the plot. Write them
   on the blackboard under the heading "Problem." Choose or have
   the students vote on which one to use. (In our story, the queen told
   the prince and princess to be careful in the swamp. When they first
   met the toad, he was rude and splashed muddy water on them
   because they were throwing stones into the water. This provided
   the first complication.)
6. Ask students for a solution. Choose or have your class vote on the
   suggestion preferred. Write the chosen solution on the blackboard
   immediately following the problem that it solves. (The class decided the royal children would be sent to bed without supper.)
7. Continue in this manner, getting a few more problems and their
   solutions from the students. (Additional problems involved the
   Toad King and the magic spell. The class decided that a wicked

witch had cast the spell. They didn't care *why*; that's what wicked witches do. With older students, I spend more time on motivation, and the "why" becomes more important. I also challenge stereotypes whenever I can. With this first-grade class, I led a little discussion about the "wicked witch" characterization. I was told by a 6-year-old, "Yes, we know all that, but this witch has to be wicked in this story. It's her job." I yielded to this logic. The class did care *how* the spell could be broken. They decided that a fierce dragon would have to be killed to break the spell. I intervened for the dragon at this point. I said that instead of being killed, the dragon had to be tamed without being hurt. I just don't like violence, and I figure I'm the storyteller, so I'm allowed to make the rules.)

8. Interrupt the story just after a major problem has been added. Tell the students they will finish the story themselves. Our story was interrupted after the problem of the dragon was added.

9. Spend 5 or 10 minutes getting suggestions for possible endings, listing them on the blackboard under "Solutions." This will help the less imaginative students to get ideas and will spark the imaginations of the more creative students. (Some of the suggestions in this case were the following: "Use magic." "Feed him and he'll become a pet." "Trick him." "Yell at him and scare him." "Give him something he really wants." "Sing him a song.")

10. Either allow time in class to finish the story or assign it as homework. Older students can write their stories and add illustrations if desired. Younger children can draw or paint their ideas and tell their endings to the teacher, who can print each student's ideas on his or her pictures.

11. Share the stories in class.

Variation

▩ After you and your class have played this story game a few times, you may want to omit the use of the blackboard. In that case, the students will not be voting for which suggestion they want to be used in the story; you will have to make all the choices. When I use this variation, I will say, "These are wonderful ideas. I would like to use them all, but I have to choose one. If your idea wasn't used, you can put it in your own story when you retell this one." Sometimes I will use an option that no one has suggested, if I can think of one.

Hint

◼ Don't interrupt the story too soon. Give your students time enough to become invested in the story and the characters and to experience solving a few problems first.

Scrambled 1-2-3

Time estimate: 20 to 60 minutes. Can be done in two or more sessions.
Suggested grade level: 4 through 12
Level of difficulty: Intermediate
Preparation: Art supplies

Comments

This activity is a natural sequence to Basic 1-2-3 (see p. 49), which grades above 4 can skip and begin with this one. Like Basic 1-2-3, it uses a visual art form to teach storytelling basics but requires more creativity and an understanding of the three basics of story line. This entertaining activity also has been enjoyed by my college classes.

Procedure

1. Assign the numbers 1, 2, or 3 to each student. Tell them they will be drawing or painting either the beginning, middle, or end of the story they will hear, according to the number each has been assigned.
2. Read or tell a story to the class.
3. Have the students draw or paint a picture that represents the part of the story line that matches their assigned number. In other words, Number 1s will make a picture about the beginning and so on.
4. Review the three main parts of a story (see pp. 45-46).
5. Select a picture from each group and rearrange their sequence to 2-3-1. In other words, Number 2's picture becomes the beginning, Number 3's the middle, and Number 1's the ending of the story.
6. Ask the class to create a new story, using the rearranged pictures. They will use whatever is depicted on Number 2's picture

to begin the story, introducing character, setting, and purpose.
Number 3's picture will be used to generate the conflict, and Number 1's will help provide the solution. This procedure should generate a very different story from the original one. An example follows
this activity.

7. Repeat steps 5 and 6, using a 3-1-2 sequence.
8. Repeat steps 5 and 6, using a 3-2-1 sequence.

Variation

 ▧ After steps 5 through 8 have been done as a group activity, form
triads of students so that there is a 1, 2, and 3 in each group. Ask
the groups to generate their own stories by rearranging sequences.
These stories can be written down and shared with the rest of the
class.

Hint

 ▧ Pictures can be hung on a clothesline for easy rearranging.

Example

In one of my classes, we told the fable of "The Fox and the Crow."
In this story, the crow has a large piece of cheese and refuses to share it
with the hungry fox. The fox flatters the crow and tricks it into dropping
the cheese, then runs away with the cheese, leaving the crow without any.
Number 1's picture showed the crow holding the cheese in its mouth,
Number 2's showed the fox and the crow with the cheese falling, and
Number 3's showed the fox running away, leaving the crow with an
open, empty beak. When rearranged 2-3-1, the resulting story was the
following:

Story: The Fox, the Crow, and the Cheese

Once upon a time there was a fox who went around bullying
everyone who was smaller than he was. He was picking on a little
mouse, who ran away. A crow had come outside to prepare lunch.

She was carrying a big cheese to cut up, because she was expecting company. She saw the fox being mean to the little mouse and she decided to teach the fox a lesson. She dropped the big cheese right on his head. He was so scared he ran away without even looking to see what had fallen. The crow retrieved her cheese, which was no worse for having been dropped, and got ready for her company.

Moral: Bullies are cowards in disguise.

Intro to Improv

Time estimate: 15 to 60 minutes. Can be done in several sessions.
Suggested grade level: 4 through 12
Level of difficulty: Intermediate
Preparation: A cleared space for the actors

Comments

This activity is a good way to introduce creative dramatics into the classroom. It is an excellent way to teach story line basics as well as teamwork, listening skills, problem solving, and flexibility. The story is acted out before it is written down and/or told as a narrative and uses children's natural ability to play.

Procedure

1. Review the three main parts of a story (see pp. 45-46).
2. Explain to your students that they are going to act out 1-2-3 stories. Number 1 actor will start the scene with an activity such as mowing the lawn. Number 2 will provide a conflict, and Number 3 will solve it. Explain that the actors may have to let go of some of their ideas to accept new ideas and work together.
3. Assign numbers 1, 2, or 3 to each student, or ask your students to select their own numbers, provided they are equally represented.
4. Ask for a Number 1 to volunteer, or select someone. Number 1 will come to the cleared space and begin the scene, letting the class know by words and actions what activity he or she is performing. For example, the student may pantomime digging while saying, "Now to plant that tree."

5. As soon as the class guesses the activity, select a Number 2 to provide conflict or complication by joining Number 1 and making life difficult. Number 2 may say something such as, "You can't dig there! That's my property." Whichever character and ideas Number 2 offers, Number 1 accepts them and continues the scene. In this example, Number 2 seems to be a neighbor. Number 1 does not refuse this idea by saying something such as, "Who are you? I never saw you before." Number 1 accepts the idea and relates to Number 2 as a neighbor. If Number 1 had decided to be only 5 years old, he or she needs to let Number 2 know, perhaps by "crying" or saying something such as, "I'm going to tell my daddy that you yelled at me!" Then Number 2 would relate to Number 1 as if he or she were a child. If Number 1 has not let Number 2 know about this decision to be 5 years old by speech or behavior, and Number 2 says, "We've been neighbors for 30 years," then Number 1 should accept this idea and let go of the previous idea of being 5 years old. Instead of playing an angry neighbor, Number 2 might try to help Number 1 and botch matters terribly.

6. When things are hopelessly tangled, select a Number 3 to come in and solve the problem. Number 3 might say, "Why don't you plant that tree somewhere else?" or alternatively show them how to work together. Number 1 and Number 2 then let go of their conflict and accept the solution. Sometimes, students are having so much fun being adversarial that the first two actors don't want to accept any resolution. You may have to remind them to release and accept and that the three of them are supposed to be working together to tell the story.

7. Instruct your actors to take a bow and then sit down.

8. Choose a student to come forward and tell the story he or she has just seen enacted.

9. Now that the students are familiar with the procedure, repeat steps 4 through 8, using three new students and a new 1-2-3 plot.

10. Repeat until everyone has had a turn. (Instead of giving every student a turn at one session, this activity can be repeated over as many class periods as necessary. The students might benefit from having fewer stories to remember at a time.)

11. Ask your students to write one of the stories they have seen performed.

12. Share and compare stories. They can be collected in a book.

Variations

- Proceed as above. Ask students to change the ending of the play they have just seen. Share the stories in class to see how many different endings can be written to the same beginning and middle of a story.

- Proceed as above, except that after the first group has performed, have another group perform their 1-2-3. Do not stop to do any writing until everyone has had a turn. If time permits, rotate numbers until every student has had a chance to be 1, 2, and 3. Ask the students to tell or write the play they liked best, changing the ending if they like.

Hints

- Encourage your students to ask for suggestions from classmates if they have difficulty thinking of a character or action to perform. The students have the choice whether to accept the suggestions. I think it is better to wait for the student to ask for suggestions rather than just to offer help, because it is more empowering to ask for help than to wait and look hopeless. Tell the students before this activity begins that it is all right to ask for help. Explain to the class that if they offer suggestions without being asked, they are sending the message that they don't think their classmate will be able to handle the situation and won't be able to ask for help at the appropriate time. Try to encourage Number 1s to show what they are doing rather than to simply announce it to the class. This will help to develop accuracy and clarity.

- Sometimes, students will go beyond acceptable boundaries while improvising to test the limits of a new, relatively unstructured activity. Treat this just as you would any other inappropriate behavior.

Improv 1-2-3

Time estimate: 15 to 60 minutes. Can be done in several sessions.
Suggested grade level: 4 through 12
Level of difficulty: Intermediate
Preparation: A cleared space for the actors to perform

Comments

This is a popular theater game that teaches the spontaneity, creativity, and flexibility so necessary for improvisational acting. It also teaches students to give and take feedback without becoming defensive. It is included here because of the abilities it teaches, because it leads to the creation of stories and plays, and because it teaches basic plot structure. It is an advanced form of Intro to Improv (see p. 69) and requires more responsibility and teamwork.

The objectives of this activity, and of others in this book that use dramatization, are to teach story structure, characterization, and storytelling techniques. We are not trying to turn out finished, professional actors, although the successful, enjoyable acting experiences these activities provide may motivate students to study acting in more detail.

Your students will need the following information about responsibilities and stage movement:

Responsibilities of the Actor. For our purposes, then, an actor has four responsibilities:

1. The actor needs to be heard by the audience.
2. The actor needs to be seen by the audience.
3. The actor needs to stay in character. Once the play has started, the actor cannot ask questions or stop the action. Everything the actor does must be in character.
4. The actor needs to give and accept ideas in character during the play instead of insisting on having his or her way, thus preventing the plot from moving toward resolution.

Responsibilities of the Audience. The audience has its responsibilities, too. Besides giving the actors the courtesies of attention and applause, the audience will give positive feedback to the actors. They will tell what worked for them and what they liked. For example, instead of talking about when the actor could not be heard, they will tell when they could hear very well. They also can suggest alternate possible endings to what they have just seen.

Stage Movement. Stage movement is called *blocking.* Styles have changed over the years. The elaborate gestures that used to be considered necessary for an actor are now seen only in melodramas. Present-day audiences prefer more natural movements. There are just a few things to tell your students about stage movement:

1. Let the audience see your face. Experienced actors can convey emotion with their backs (usually with the help of a camera to provide focus by showing only the actor's back), but for our purposes, face the audience. This means that if any actor stands between you and the audience, you either move the actor or yourself within the context of the play. The only exception is when you don't want the audience's focus. Then it is helpful to turn away, let someone stand in front of you, or move upstage (see Glossary).

2. Don't take focus away from another actor. This is called *upstaging,* and it is a big no-no! It is done by moving upstage of an actor so that he or she has to turn away from the audience to see you, by standing in front of another actor, or by moving while someone else is talking. It is also done by sneezing, coughing, laughing loudly, making a large gesture, using a handkerchief, or by any other distraction you can think of. (Most upstaging is unintentional, especially with beginning actors who have not yet learned to be aware of how their movements can draw focus. Help your students to become aware of unintentional upstaging. Discourage intentional upstaging by talking about the need to work together to tell the story.)

3. Keep the stage balanced. Think of the stage as a platform resting on a central support, running front to back like a giant seesaw. Try to place yourselves so the platform won't tilt to one side. When another actor moves, you move to correct the balance within the context of the play.

4. Don't hurt one another. Avoid fight scenes whenever possible, and if one is essential to the plot, teach your actors how to "fake it." A "blow" delivered with the downstage hand looks real when the swing of the arm is continued past the chin and the recipient turns his head upstage, even though no actual contact is made. If an actor is in profile to the audience, a "slap" to the upstage side of the face will look real if the head moves as if contact has been made, even though there is no touching. Caution your students to stay aware and in control of their movements and to be gentle with one another. Sometimes students, especially in the lower grades, get carried away. It's best in this likelihood to avoid any contact whatsoever, except something such as shaking hands.

5. Don't bump into the furniture.

That's all there is. We'll leave anything else to regular acting classes.

Procedure

1. Review the three main parts to a story (see pp. 45-46).
2. Discuss the responsibilities of an actor.
3. Have each student practice speaking so that students in the back row can hear easily.
4. Have each student stand so the audience can see his or her face. Have students practice moving so they don't block other students from the audience's view.
5. Discuss the responsibilities of the audience.
6. Divide the students into triads (groups of three) and assign numbers 1, 2, and 3 within the groups.
7. Explain that Number 1s will decide who and where their characters are and will begin an action. Number 2s will choose to become characters who will complicate things and create problems, which Number 3s will solve. Allow the groups a few minutes to plan. More experienced groups will not need this planning time, as they learn to trust their own improvising abilities.
8. Review stage movement (see pp. 72-73).
9. Select a group to perform a short play as described in Intro to Improv (see p. 69) and in step 7 above.
10. When the play is over, ask the actors to take a bow and cue the audience to applaud. Instruct the actors to stay in front of the class to receive positive feedback from the audience. Remind them that any comments they receive are opinions and are neither right nor wrong. The actors do not need to defend themselves, because the choices they made were right for them at the time. They may or may not want to try it differently next time.
11. Ask the actors to sit down in the audience to watch the next group perform and receive positive feedback.
12. Continue until all groups have performed.
13. Reassign numbers within triads and continue until each student has had a turn beginning, complicating, and ending a scene.

Variation

▪ Instead of having all the groups perform in turn, let the first group perform their play again, using some of the suggestions they received from the audience. This will shorten the time needed for that session. The activity can be continued over as many days as desired. If only one play is worked on in a session, the students can write the story they have seen enacted, making any changes they would like.

Hints

- Let the students who have acted the scene give their comments before the audience starts giving feedback.
- Discourage any attempt on the part of the actors to explain or defend once the audience begins to give feedback.
- Do not allow the play to go on if the audience is restless. If talking about the responsibilities of an audience plus a gentle reminder do not work, change the activity so that you do not give your students practice in being inattentive or rude to one another.

The following 1-2-3 was created by three fifth-grade students.

Story: Fishing

The scene opens in a woods by a stream. A young woman is fishing in the stream. A little girl is playing ball noisily nearby. The woman keeps asking her to be quiet, but the child keeps making noise.

The woman takes the ball away from the child. She says she will give it back if the little girl will go somewhere else with it. Instead, the girl starts asking if she can help the woman with her fishing.

The woman refuses and tells the girl to stop bothering her. Just then, a fish bites on the line, and the woman starts to reel it in.

The child gets excited. "Let me do it!" she yells. She grabs the fishing rod out of the woman's hands and pulls the fish out of the water.

A game warden walks up and asks the child for her fishing license. "Oh," she says, "I'm not fishing; that lady is."

The warden said, "Then how come you have the fishing rod and the fish?" and he gave the little girl a ticket for fishing without a license.

The End

Creative Dramatics 1-2-3

Time estimate: 60 minutes daily for 2 to 4 weeks
Suggested grade level: 4 through 12, although some advanced third
　　graders can do this activity
Level of difficulty: Advanced
Preparation: Cleared space for actors to perform. You may want to
　　use costumes, props, and so on, but they are not necessary.

Comments

This is a good way to create an original play in the classroom. It is
an excellent way to expand and enrich a unit in social studies or psychology and ensures student involvement with the material. We recommend
that you wait until students are familiar with Improv 1-2-3 (see p. 71)
before introducing this advanced activity.

Procedure

1. Review the basic parts of a story, stage movement, and the responsibilities of actors and audience (see p. 72).
2. Choose a topic for improvisation, such as drug abuse or the Civil
   War, or one of the short plays developed during one of the other
   activities. If possible, let the class choose which subject they want
   to expand into a play. The example given at the end of this activity
   deals with an issue that was chosen by a sixth-grade class using
   this activity. The play was performed for an invited audience,
   using minimal costuming, makeup, and set.
3. Divide the students into triads and assign numbers 1, 2, and 3
   within the groups.
4. Ask Number 1 to begin an appropriate action, asking for suggestions if necessary. (In our example, Number 1 decided to portray
   an older woman working in her garden and admiring her flowers.)
5. Ask Number 2 to decide on a character who will complicate the
   plot. (Our Number 2 told Number 1, "This garden will have to go.
   I'm surveyor for the company that's going to build 500 low-cost
   housing units right here." Number 1 protested, "You can't do that!
   I have my rights, you know." They began to argue heatedly.)
6. Ask Number 3 to decide on a character who will resolve the situation. (Our Number 3 said, "Now folks, don't fight. As your

mayor, I'm going to call a special town meeting, where everyone will be heard.")

7. When the play is over, ask the actors to take a bow while the audience applauds. The actors stay in front of the class for positive feedback from the audience, as in Improv 1-2-3. Ask, "What changes could we make? This was good—how can it be better?"

8. Audience members who have suggestions for different endings or different characterizations are asked to replace one or more of the actors and replay the story, with their suggested changes.

9. Add characters to the play. (In our example, many townspeople, all with their own agendas, were added.)

10. Make the play longer and more complex. What happened before the scene started? What happens after the scene ends? What did the hero tell his friends? What did they say? After each scene, get feedback. How could it be better?

11. Continue adding characters and action. Have students exchange and play all parts. This is important. Not only will it yield ideas for expanding the plot and fleshing out the characters, but it will ensure capable substitutes for when students are absent.

12. Put an outline, or scenario, of the play the class has developed on the board with a list of characters.

13. Have students choose the characters they would prefer to portray. You may have to intervene, but usually the students work things out for themselves. The play can be double- or triple-cast, with two or three students taking turns portraying the same character.

14. Have students develop their characters by using the Character Description Forms (see Resources).

15. Continue to develop the play. Introduce the concept of motivation. Ask, "What was your character doing before the action started? What does your character hope to accomplish and how? How does your character feel about the others in the play? What happens next, and how does it affect your character?" The Character Description Forms will help to answer these questions. Ask the students to incorporate their answers into the play.

16. Continue rehearsal, always asking, "What worked? How could it be better?"

17. In 2 to 4 weeks you will have a finished play ready to perform. There will be no lines to remember, and everyone will know every part. I do want to stress that it is the process of developing the play that has been important, whether or not the play ever is performed

before an audience. Undue emphasis on the end product increases tension and anxiety and hampers creativity.

18. Your students may want to add costumes, makeup, props, and scenery, or even music and dance. This could really get big, with posters, programs, and an invited audience. The play could be videotaped, shown on cable, or toured and used as a fund-raiser. Other classes, such as homemaking, art, chorus, orchestra, physical education, carpentry, printshop, and video can be involved. Several touring drug education plays started in this manner.

Hints

- Encourage your students to "keep it real" instead of overacting. Point out that there are no mistakes; just make whatever happens (or doesn't happen) a part of the play.
- If you can matter of factly have boys and girls switch roles, you will reap the incidental benefit of increased gender awareness and understanding. If your class is too silly about it, don't insist.

Because there never was a script for the play that follows, I wrote it in narrative form for inclusion in this book. Performance time was about 10 minutes.

Play: The Town Meeting

Scenario

1. Mayor in square. Meeting about housing development today. Hurry.
2. Men in park arguing for and against.
3. Children in, pester men.
4. Enter lovers, children tease them, then leave.
5. Frustrated courtship.
6. Children in, tease lovers, get money and go, but bump into women, then off.
7. Women complain.
8. Mayor in, makes speech, off.
9. People into courthouse, talking about mayor.

The Town Meeting

Mayor Jones was hurrying across the town square to his office. Today was going to be very exciting. The townspeople were meeting today to decide whether to allow a big company to come in and build 500 low-cost housing units to be occupied by people from out of state. It was a hot issue, and there were many different factions.

The mayor looked around the square with satisfaction, nodding at the statue of his great-great-grandfather. Then he checked his watch and hurried into the town hall to make sure someone had started the coffee.

A group of men were sitting in the park, waiting for meeting time. They were arguing about the advantages and disadvantages of the issue. One man, Joe, thought the people should be allowed to move in. He offered as argument that the old people would have someone to talk to while the younger ones were at work. Another man, Al, was afraid of what would happen to the wildlife. An old man shook his head, "The only wildlife I'm interested in is some faster women. All these old women around here do is rest and tend their gardens."

The men laughed, and one of them said, "But I like the town the way it is. We'll lose our small-town atmosphere if we let those people in." The arguments continued: There would be more jobs, but the farmers would have to move. But if the newcomers were kept out, wasn't that a violation of their freedom?

Three children ran over and began pestering the men, interrupting them and chasing one another noisily. The men tried to chase them away, but the children only increased their noise.

The teasing stopped only when the children found new victims. An attractive young woman named Christy entered the square, followed by two young men, Ed and Mark, desperately competing for her attention. The children formed a circle around the three and began chanting:

"Three little lovebirds sitting in a tree, K-I-S-S-I-N-G. First comes love, second comes marriage, third comes a baby in the baby carriage."

Finally, the children tired of their sport and left the three alone to talk. The two young men kept trying to flatter and agree with Christy, but she wasn't giving them much help. She said, "Maybe we should let these people come into our town." Ed hastened to agree. "Yes, Christy, you're never wrong."

"Everybody's wrong some time," she replied, and Mark agreed. "What?" Christy asked, "Are you saying I'm always wrong?" Ed pressed his advantage, "That's what Mark said. Oh Christy, your hair is so pretty. Did you just come from the beauty shop?" Christy answered, "Are you saying I need to go?"

The men gave up trying to use words, and each took one of her arms, pulling her in opposite directions. She got mad at both of them. Just then the children resumed their teasing. Ed gave them some money to go away and they ran off, only to bump into a group of older women who were coming to the meeting. Sheepishly, the children ran off, with the women scolding them.

"Inconsiderate little brats!" they grumbled. "First they disturb our nap time and then they run into us! And if all these new people come in, it will be even worse. They'll make lots of noise, run all over our gardens, and leave their trash all over the place."

They were interrupted by Mayor Jones coming out of the town hall. He greeted all the people and made a speech urging them to vote to allow the housing units to be built. "I know you'll do the right thing," he said, "and now if you'll all come in, we can begin the meeting."

He went back into the building, and one of the old women said loudly, "He's just trying to line his own pockets." "That's right," said one of the working men, "I know for a fact he's giving a big contract to his own brother."

The people started into the building, still grumbling. One of them said, "You know, before we discuss the new housing units, we ought to talk about maybe getting a new mayor." A lot of agreement was heard as the crowd filed into the building.

The End

TABLE 4.1 Grade-Level Guidelines: Story Lines

	K-12	*PK-2*	*3-5*	*6-12*
Circle Story	X			
Unfinished Story	X			
Basic 1-2-3		X	X	
Mixed-Up Start-Up			X	X
Round Robin	X			
Pocket Robin			X	X
Surprise Robin			X	X
Touchie-Feelie Robin			X	X
Mystery Robin				X
Group Storybuilding	X			
Storybuilding 1-2	X			
Scrambled 1-2-3			X	X
Intro to Improv			X	X
Improv 1-2-3			X	X
Creative Dramatics 1-2-3			X	X

5

Description and Characterization

Now that your students have learned the basics of story line construction, all that remains is to teach them how to add substance and color through description and characterization.

Description is a way to add enriching detail to a story to help the listener experience it more fully. A good way to start teaching the use of description is to have your students tell a story and then ask them to retell it, adding sensory words. The students will see for themselves how much more interesting their stories become when they add the rustle of leaves or the icy cold shock of water as the hero dives into a rushing mountain stream.

Characterization includes such things as motives, emotions, attitudes, behavior, intelligence, background, status, past history, physical attributes, inner dialogue, and spoken conversation. One of the best ways to develop characterization is through point of view (POV) activities. Few stories describe events as they are seen through the eyes of all the characters. Stories told in first person announce their POV clearly, and most stories told in third person usually have only one POV—that of the main character or of the writer.

Students need to consider viewpoints other than that of the main character. This increased understanding carries over to interpersonal relationships in real life. Often, a POV activity will provide students with their first experience of putting themselves in someone else's place. Once they grasp the concept that not everyone feels the same way, they can begin to apply that new understanding to their interpersonal relationships. Intercultural tolerance and acceptance increase to the extent that we can appreciate other points of view.

Even more important is the realization that we are not so different from one another after all. This leads to acceptance of others and to self-acceptance as well.

All POV activities can be dramatized easily by using the insights into character and motivation that have been learned. This dramatization can be as simple or complex as desired. It can be done without any costuming, props, or sets or with just a simple symbolic object, such as a hat or a candle. In fact, it can be done without any props at all by using pantomime to indicate needed objects. Students can bring costumes and props from home or make them in class, or entire departments can be involved in a large-scale production. I prefer to keep it simple.

A possible exception would be the dramatization of a historical story. The activity could be expanded to include research on clothing, architecture, means of travel, events occurring at that time, and anything else pertinent. The Character Description Forms (see Resources) will help your students benefit from the activities in this chapter.

In summary, description adds dimension to the listener's experience and enriches the story. POV activities help to broaden awareness and appreciation of differences and similarities between people. They increase understanding and personal involvement in the subject being studied. They are excellent for use with social studies, psychology, multicultural classes, or any time you want the students to "walk in someone else's moccasins."

Add-a-Sense

Time estimate: 15 to 20 minutes
Suggested grade level: 3 through 12

Level of difficulty: Beginning
Preparation: None

Comments

This activity will help to show how description can enrich a story.

Procedure

1. Ask your students to choose partners and to sit facing them.
2. Designate which one is to tell a story first. (The tallest one? The one closest to the windows?)
3. Choose a story topic, such as "A Halloween I'll Always Remember." Almost any subject listed under Me, Myself, and Others (see Chapter 2) will work.
4. Ask the first student to tell a story about the chosen topic to his or her partner. Allow 3 to 5 minutes.
5. Ask the second student to tell a story to his or her partner, again allowing 3 to 5 minutes.
6. Ask your students to name the five senses. Write them on the board using them as headings. Elicit sensory words from your students and write them on the board under the appropriate headings.
7. Ask the first student to tell his or her original story again, this time adding words that have to do with the senses. Direct the student to add a sensory word wherever feasible, referring to the lists on the board if necessary.
8. Repeat step 7 with the second student.
9. Discuss the activity with your class. Ask the students what, if any, difference it made to add sensory words to the story.
10. Tell your students to write down the second story they told.
11. Have partners switch papers and underline or highlight every descriptive word.
12. Switch papers and have students check their papers to see what was highlighted.

Variation

▪ Have students add words that describe actions as in step 7. Remind them to describe behavior and actions instead of simply stating inner dialogue and feelings. For example, instead of stating that the hero was worried, the student can have him pace, lick his lips, look out the window repeatedly, and so on.

Point of View

Time estimate: 15 to 30 minutes
Suggested grade level: 4 through 12
Level of difficulty: Intermediate
Preparation: Duplicated Character Description Forms (see Resources)

Comments

This is not an introductory storytelling activity and usually is done as a follow-up to a story that already has been told or assigned. It is an excellent way to teach the punctuation and form of conversational writing.

Procedure

1. Read, tell, or assign a story, or use one that already has been created by the students.
2. Familiarize students with the Character Description Forms. Use whichever form fits your purpose and the abilities of your students.
3. Discuss the characters in the story, using the questions on the Character Description Forms.
4. Ask one of the students to retell the story from the point of view of one of the characters other than the main one in the story.
5. Continue in this manner until viewpoints of all the characters have been explored.
6. Discuss the activity.

Variations

▨ Assign a different character to each student. (You may have to double up if you have more students than characters.) Have students write the story from their assigned character's viewpoint. This can be done as a homework assignment. Share the completed stories and discuss in class.

- Choose a nursery rhyme or a familiar children's story and proceed as described above. The characters are usually simple stereotypes, which makes it easier for younger students to do this activity. It is a lot of fun, and older students enjoy it, too.
- Choose a historical novel or a nonfiction history book and proceed as described. This is an excellent way to make history come alive and increase student involvement in the subject.
- Have students write letters to the characters in the story, with each student writing to a different character. Share with the class.
- Have students write a diary or "A day in the life of . . ." as one of the characters, with each student writing as a different character. Share with the class.
- Have students write a letter as a character in the story might, with each student writing as a different character. Share with the class.
- Animals, insects, or inanimate objects can be personified and given a voice and a point of view. Such unlikely things as leaves or blood corpuscles can be given a voice, as in "I am Joe's heart."
- Substitute famous people—living or dead, real or fictional—for the characters in the story. Keeping the portrayals realistic for both the story and also the substituted person should be quite a challenge and should yield some interesting results.
- Switch the good and bad characters and rewrite the story. For example, Oliver Twist could be evil and dishonest, and Fagin could be a good-hearted person who is trying to help him. With this variation, you can challenge stereotypes and often show how some authors reveal their biases through characterizations.
- Tell or write the same story from two POVs—for example, a story about a boy teaching his dog to "fetch." The student would tell it first from the boy's POV and then from the dog's.

Hint

- If your students have difficulty imagining what another's POV might be, remind them that all of us tend to believe we are the heroes of our own stories, and we consider anyone who stops us from getting what we want as either bad, mean, stupid, or misguided.

Panel Point of View

Time estimate: 15 to 20 minutes
Suggested grade level: 2 through 12
Level of difficulty: Intermediate
Preparation: Table with chairs in performing area

Comments

In this POV activity, characters from nursery rhymes, cartoons, comic strips, or other one-dimensional characters such as Rambo are interviewed by a host on a panel show. Panel members can be mixed or matched. For example, they could all be Mother Goose characters, or Bo Peep could appear with Goldilocks and Superman. Students answer and interact as their characters would in "reality." Although this activity seems difficult, I have found that second graders do very well with it.

Procedure

1. Tell the students they are going to have a panel show. Ask who has seen one on television.
2. Help the class to decide what kind of guests will be interviewed—nursery rhyme characters, heroes, movie stars, and so on.
3. Choose students to play the host and the characters. The remaining students will be the studio audience.
4. Let the "guests" choose their own characters. Remind them to stay with their characters' POV rather than try to be funny by breaking character.
5. Discuss the types of questions the host might ask. Write some suggestions on the blackboard. (The host may opt not to use these suggestions.)
6. Ask the actors to begin the panel show. The host will interview the first guest, who will reply in character.
7. As the guests finish, they can join the studio audience and another guest can be chosen, or the first guest can stay to interact with the other guests.
8. Replace the host as desired.
9. Continue until everyone has performed.

Variations

- ▓ Choose guests who already have a history of conflict with one another, such as the wolf and the three little pigs or Goldilocks and the three bears. They will get to tell their stories from their own POV while the host tries to keep peace.
- ▓ Have the guests keep their identity a secret. The host will have to ask questions to find out who they are. If the host guesses who a guest is, that character is replaced. If the host fails to guess in a specified length of time, he or she is replaced.
- ▓ A co-host can be chosen to share the interviewing.

Alibi Point of View

Time estimate: 15 to 20 minutes
Suggested grade level: K through 12
Level of difficulty: Beginning/intermediate
Preparation: Clear space for actors to perform

Comments

This dramatization technique is good for very young students, although older students also enjoy it. One of the characters in the story is double-cast. The first of the two actors will be in the dramatized version of a familiar story that sticks pretty close to the original. The other actor becomes the narrator, who stands to one side of the "stage" and tells quite a different version in which he or she is blameless and heroic. The narrator does not have to stick to the truth and can be as outrageous as it is feasible. Although the narrator does not see or hear the characters, the characters occasionally may hear and react to what the narrator is saying.

Procedure

1. Read or tell a familiar child's story or fairy tale, such as "Goldilocks and the Three Bears." Be sure that everyone is familiar with the story you are going to use.
2. Ask the class how the individual characters might view the events of the story. For example, Momma Bear might see Goldilocks as a spoiled brat who went into a house when no one was home, ate

food without asking permission, generally made herself at home, and carelessly broke the baby's chair. Goldilocks, on the other hand, might tell things differently, especially if she doesn't have to stick to the facts stated or implied in the story.

3. Explain to the students that some of them will act out the familiar story while the narrator tells another version that may be different. This narrator will stand off to one side and tell his or her story while the other actors perform the action "unnoticed." If desired, the actors can react with disbelief or outrage to some of the narrator's statements and then return to the play as if they hadn't stopped. Remember, you will need two actors for the hero—one to narrate and the other to be in the play.

4. Review the responsibilities of actors and audience and the basics of stage movement (see Chapter 4).

5. Cast the characters, asking for volunteers or making assignments. Those students not selected will be the audience.

6. Ask the chosen actors to perform as described in step 3.

7. When the play is over, instruct actors to bow and accept applause from the audience, followed by positive feedback about the performance.

8. Ask your students to write what they have seen performed, either in play script or narrative form.

Variations

- Instead of doing step 8, cast different students as the characters and narrator and proceed as above. Repeat until everyone has had a turn, using the same character as the narrator.
- Make another character the narrator, which will change the play accordingly.
- Short scenes using nursery rhymes can be done in a similar manner. Perhaps Miss Muffet's spider, the piper's son Tom, or Little Boy Blue would like to tell their sides of the story.

Hints

- If very young children are performing the play, dialogue can be very limited or pantomime can be used. The only spoken part of any length, that of the narrator, can be read by the teacher or an older student. In fact, if this play is performed for an invited audience, the narrator can be reading from a book. A fifth-grade class devised and performed the following play using this activity. The narrator was the Big Bad Wolf, who read from a book titled *The True Story of Red Rotten Hood.* Actions performed by the characters are indicated.

Play: The True Story of Red Rotten Hood

Narrator: Once I lived in a big woods. I filled my days by helping all my fellow creatures and baking cookies to give away to all the little children.

Action: Wolf chases some small animals, trying to eat them. They barely escape. He steals a cookie from a child, who runs away crying.

Narrator: There was a little girl named Red Riding Hood, who lived nearby. She was a terrible person. In fact, some people called her "Little Red Rotten Hood." She threw rocks at the forest creatures and was mean to everyone.

Action: Red Riding Hood pets the animals. They obviously like her.

Narrator: Even her mother didn't like her. She was especially mean to her poor old Grandma, one of my favorite foods—I mean—friends. One day I heard Red Rotten Hood's mother tell her to go help her poor old Grandma. Red Rotten Hood didn't want to, and they had a big fight, which Red Rotten Hood lost.

Action: Mother calls Red Riding Hood, smiles sweetly at her, and asks her to take basket of cookies to Grandma. Red Riding Hood expresses concern about Grandma and says she will stay and read to her.

Narrator: I thought I'd better go warn Granny and help her hide, so Red Rotten Hood couldn't hurt her again. I met Red Rotten Hood on the way to Granny's. As usual, she was very rude.

Action: Wolf meets Red Riding Hood and asks where she is going. Red Riding Hood answers politely and asks him if he would like a cookie. He rudely grabs a handful and crams them into his mouth.

Narrator: I tried to think of a way to delay Red Rotten Hood so I would have time to warn Granny. I directed her the long way to Granny's house to give me a head start.

Action: Wolf directs Red Riding Hood to the "short cut."

Narrator: I knew it was wrong to tell a lie, but it was for Granny's good, so I forced myself to fib a little. I raced to Granny's house and told her to hide in the cellar.

Action: Wolf gains entrance to Granny's house and tries to catch her. She escapes and runs down into the cellar, locking the door behind her. He angrily pounds on the door until he hears Red Riding Hood coming.

Narrator: I locked the door to the cellar just in time. I heard Red Rotten Hood coming, and I decided to teach her a lesson. I disguised myself as Granny and got into her bed. I planned to scare Red Rotten Hood by saying "Boo!" if she started to hit me—me, that is, dressed as Granny.

Action: Red Riding Hood goes through classic "What big eyes you have, Granny" routine and so on. The wolf jumps out, saying, "The better to eat you with, my dear" and begins chasing her around the room. Red Riding Hood yells for help.

Narrator: My harmless little prank would have worked, too, if it hadn't been for a certain nosy woodcutter. He was always jealous of me, because the animals liked me better than they liked him. He happened to hear Red Rotten Hood and me playing our little game, and he couldn't stand being left out. He forced his way in and spoiled everything.

Action: Woodcutter rescues Red Riding Hood and warns the wolf to get out of the forest and never to return. The wolf runs away. The woodcutter and Red Riding Hood tell Granny the wolf is gone. She comes up from the cellar and everyone rejoices.

Narrator: So, you see, due to the jealousy and meanness of others, I am looking for a new place to live. Sometimes it just doesn't pay to try to help people.

The End

Point of View Aside

Time estimate: 10 to 60 minutes. Can be done in several sessions.
Suggested grade level: 4 through 12

Level of difficulty: Intermediate/advanced

Preparation: Clear space for actors to perform; duplicated Character Description Forms

Comments

This activity uses the acting technique of *aside* to teach students about developing characters and understanding motivations. An aside is a stage movement often used in melodramas. After speaking lines, the actor moves toward the audience and speaks directly to them. The other actors do not respond to what is said or even appear to hear it. All other action stops until the actor returns to his or her original position, and then the play resumes. This activity also helps to develop the ability to create realistic words for story characters to speak. It is excellent for psychology classes, because it raises the issues of vulnerability and public and private masks. Point of View Aside is not recommended for beginning or younger students. No matter how skillful and tactful you are, sometimes this activity can be threatening to some students. If the story hits too close to home, a student may be reluctant to see another character's viewpoint. If this occurs, give the student permission either to stay in the audience or choose a different character.

Procedure

1. Read, tell, or assign a story. This can be a student-generated story.
2. Select a scene if the story is too long. Using input from the class, write a scenario outline of the selected scene or story on the board.
3. Ask your class to discuss the characters, using the questions on the Character Description Forms (see Resources) as a starting point.
4. Explain the uses of an aside on stage and that asides will be used in this activity to tell what a character really is thinking or feeling. Discuss the differences between our public masks and our private ones.
5. Cast the play, asking for volunteers or assigning each character to a student. Those students not selected will be the audience.
6. Discuss the responsibilities of actors and audience and review stage movement (see Chapter 4).
7. Review the scenario. Make sure each actor knows what to do.

8. Have the students improvise the scene or story, referring to the scenario on the board as necessary. Instruct them to interrupt themselves when appropriate and to give asides about their real feelings and thoughts, which they must try to hide from the other characters. Explain that their spoken words to other characters may be quite different from those spoken in the asides.

9. Discuss the activity and how it felt to drop the public mask and reveal the private one. Talk about the circumstances when a public mask might be appropriate.

10. Repeat the activity, assigning new actors as the characters and asking the former actors to join the audience. If one scene from the story has been enacted, you might want to choose another scene to do. However, the students will not object to repeating the same scenario. It will be different each time it is performed and will hold their interest until everyone has had a turn.

Variation

* Assign characters to students and have each one complete Character Description Forms about their character as a homework assignment. Homework could be shared in class and/or students could lead the discussion about their assigned character. This will better prepare them for the activity. Proceed as above.

Shadow Point of View

Time estimate: 10 to 60 minutes. Can be done in several sessions.
Suggested grade level: 4 through 12
Level of difficulty: Intermediate/advanced
Preparation: Clear space for actors to perform; duplicated Character Description Forms

Comments

This activity uses the acting technique of *shadowing* to teach students about developing characters and understanding motivations. In shadowing, one actor speaks and acts as his or her character would in the story. A second actor immediately speaks and behaves as he or she thinks the character "actually" is feeling and thinking. The first actor behaves as if this "inner dialogue" were true, regardless of his or her original ideas, but tries to hide this "truth" from the other characters.

This activity helps to teach the creation of realistic and appropriate dialogue for the characters to speak. It teaches flexibility, sensitivity, and awareness of other viewpoints. This activity is not recommended for beginning or younger students. Even more advanced students occasionally will become upset if their "shadows" hit too close to home and express their innermost thoughts or thoughts they are afraid of. I am sure you know how to handle that eventuality, but I would be remiss if I didn't warn you.

Procedure

1. Read, tell, or assign a story. This can be a student-generated story.
2. Discuss the action of the story or selected scene to be enacted. Using input from the class, write a scenario outline on the board.
3. Discuss the characters, using the questions on the Character Description Forms (see Resources) as a starting point.
4. Explain the concept of shadowing and that it will be used in this activity to indicate what the character might really be thinking or feeling. As in Point of View Aside (see p. 91), discuss the difference between public masks and private masks.
5. Cast the play, asking for volunteers or selecting students for each character and for each shadow, making the audience out of those students not selected.
6. Discuss the responsibilities of actors and audience and review stage movement (see Chapter 4).
7. Review the scenario. Make sure all actors know what they are to do.
8. Direct the students to improvise the story or selected scene, referring to the scenario as necessary. Explain that after each speech, the actors should "freeze" while their shadows are speaking. Emphasize that the actors need to accept as truth for their characters whatever the shadows say, regardless of preconceptions, but that the actors should try to hide this "truth" from the other characters. The shadowing will slow the action down a little, but interest will be high.
9. After the performance, discuss the activity and ask the actors how it felt to have someone else decide what their characters were

thinking. Was it difficult to release preconceptions of their characters' thoughts and to accept ideas from the shadows?

10. Repeat the activity with new actors until everyone has had a turn. You might want to choose another scene, or you can repeat the one already enacted.

Variations

※ Assign characters and have students complete the Character Description Forms as homework. This will better prepare them for the activity. Proceed as above.

※ Assign characters and shadows. Have each pair work together to complete Character Description Forms on their character before the activity is done in class. It is hoped that this will bring them more into agreement and help the shadows to be more sensitive. Proceed as above.

Hint

※ Students may be reluctant to release their own preconceptions about their characters' thoughts and feelings when the shadow says something different than they have planned. They may be so attached to their own ideas or so identified with the character that any attempted change may be felt as invalidation. If that happens, they may become defensive and insistent on their own interpretation, and a power struggle may ensue. If a reminder to release and accept does not work, they may not be ready for this activity. Some review work with Improv 1-2-3 (see Chapter 4) should help.

Jury Trial Point of View

Time estimate: 2 weeks duration. Much of this activity is done as homework.

Suggested grade level: 6 through 12

Level of difficulty: Advanced

Preparation: Classroom set up as a courtroom with areas for judge, litigants, and so on; duplicated Character Description Forms

Comments

Before this activity is attempted, the class should be familiar with the story to be used and with courtroom procedures. This activity helps to develop characters and plot further than the assigned story took them. One or more of the characters are held accountable for their actions in the story and are given a jury trial. The outcome of that trial will be determined by the evidence presented in court and by the jury's decision. This is an excellent way to combine units on language arts and social studies.

This activity is best done at the end of a unit in which a book has been read in class or assigned. It is not recommended for lower grades. My experience has been that the lower grades do not understand courtroom procedures well enough to make this activity interesting or fun for them.

Procedure

1. Review the story to be sure everyone is familiar with it.
2. Read steps 2 through 8 of these procedures to the class and make sure they know what they are going to do.
3. Assign characters or ask for volunteers. You will need to cast all the characters who were alive at the end of the story. In addition, you will need to cast a judge, prosecuting attorney, defendant's lawyer, bailiff, and a jury. The rest of the students can be spectators at the trial. Some of the courtroom personnel also can be characters from the story, if appropriate.
4. All actors, including jury and spectators, will fill out Character Description Forms (see Resources). Lawyers also will gather evidence and plan strategy and will need to find and question any witnesses. Perhaps, with your approval, they will be able to discover some witnesses who were not in the book. Your sense of fairness will help you decide whether to approve a new witness character. Remember that both the prosecution and defense must be informed of all witnesses and must be able to interview them— no surprises! All of this can be assigned as homework.
5. Have your students begin the trial. It may take several days as witnesses testify and evidence is presented. Encourage everyone to stay in character during the activity.
6. The jury will select a foreman when the trial is over and will go to a separate area where they can't be overheard. While the jury is

deliberating, the spectators can discuss the case and vote on what they think the verdict will be.

7. When the jury has reached a decision, the foreman will announce the verdict.
8. The actors will react to the verdict and finish the play, still in character.
9. Discuss the activity.

Variation

▨ Choose a nursery rhyme and bring one of the characters to trial. For example, Tom, the piper's son, could be brought to court for stealing a pig. This is still an upper-grade activity.

Creative Dramatics Point of View

Time estimate: 3 to 4 weeks of 1-hour daily sessions
Suggested grade level: 3 through 12
Level of difficulty: Advanced
Preparation: Clear area for actors to perform; costumes, props, and so on may be used but are not essential; duplicated Character Description Forms

Comments

In Creative Dramatics 1-2-3 (see Chapter 4), students created an original play starting from a story line. Here is another way to create an original play in the classroom, starting from characterization. The characters used can relate to a unit being studied or can be chosen by the students according to preference and interest. I recommend that you wait until students are familiar with both POV and 1-2-3 activities before introducing this advanced activity.

Procedure

1. Review the basic parts of a story and discuss character POV (see pp. 82-83).
2. Tell the students they are going to make up an original play. Ask them to choose a character they would like to portray and to fill

out Character Description Forms about that character. This can be assigned as homework.

3. Write the characters' names and/or descriptions on the board. (In the example given below, a fifth-grade class that developed the play furnished the following list: Jesse James, Billy the Kid, Tell Sackett, a Martian, a queen, a princess, two rodeo queens, two male rodeo stars, a sheriff, a deputy sheriff, a dog, and three punk teenagers.)

4. Discuss what setting would accommodate all the characters. (The fifth-grade class decided they could use all the characters, with very little modification, in a small western town like their own.)

5. Ask for suggestions as to what actions and motivations the listed characters might have and how they would interact with one another. Continue taking suggestions until a tentative scenario is developed. Write the scenario on the board.

6. Review the responsibilities of actors and audience and review stage movement (see pp. 72-73).

7. Break the scenario into very small segments for improvisation.

8. Ask the students whose chosen characters are involved to improvise the first small segment while the rest of the class serves as the audience.

9. When the performance is over, ask for positive feedback, first from the actors and then from the audience. Ask, "What worked? How could it be better? What else needs to happen?"

10. Ask the actors to repeat the first segment, using some of the suggestions given.

11. Get feedback again, as in step 9.

12. Go on to the next small segment, repeating steps 8 through 11.

13. Continue in this manner until every segment has been performed. This may take 2 or more days to complete.

14. Repeat steps 8 through 13, encouraging your students to expand the segments and to start joining them together into larger segments. Remind your students that they will have to develop smooth transitions between segments.

15. Form small groups of characters who are in the same segments of the play and have them work together. Assign each small group a different location so the groups won't distract one another.

16. Bring the groups together to perform what they have devised. Those not in the segment being performed will be the audience and will give positive feedback.
17. Gradually put segments together until they form actual scenes.
18. By the end of the first week, do a complete run-through without stopping, even if some of the scenes are not complete yet. Your students need to experience the continuity of the whole play. Instruct them to improvise whatever they need to do to get through the whole play.
19. Break up the play again into scenes or smaller segments and direct the students to continue working through the segments as described above. A complete run-through of the play should be done at least once a week during the rehearsal process and every day during the week before the performance.
20. The play can be performed for other classes, for an invited audience, or toured. Costumes can be as simple or as complicated as desired. Other classes, such as art, carpentry, printing, and homemaking, can be involved. If costumes and makeup are to be used, there should be a dress rehearsal the day before the performance.

Hint

- Because the entire play is improvised around a scenario, there are no lines to learn. The entire class has watched and/or acted in every rehearsal and has helped to develop the play, so every student is familiar with every part. This means that if someone is sick, another student can step into the part. Every teacher has a horror story about his or her lead actor getting sick or having to go out of town on the day of performance. This can be a disaster with a scripted show but is handled easily and skillfully by students who have created their own play through improvisation. Because no script ever was written for the following play, it has been written in narrative form for inclusion in this book. The play was performed for an invited audience and videotaped. The kids were great and the audience loved it.

Play: Big Trouble in a Little Town

Scenario

1. Time warp. Jesse James, Billy the Kid, Tell Sackett, and Jok-Tar. Going to take over town.
2. Punks, going to take over town, meet first four, form gang.
3. Committee meeting, arguments.
4. Gang arrives, welcomed, puts guns away.
5. Gunfighters pair off with women, Jok-Tar changes puppy. Townsmen object.
6. Teenagers object, are scared off.
7. Happy ending/beginning.

Big Trouble in a Little Town

It looked like any little town in the Oregon high desert, with one small difference. Over a bunch of saw grass just outside of town, the air began to shimmer, like the sun shining on a curtain of fine spider webs. Suddenly, a man in a worn cowboy outfit fell through the curtain of light. He looked around him as if dazed.

Immediately behind him came two more men, similarly dressed. They looked at one another warily and then with recognition. One said, pointing at the other two, "You're Jesse James and Billy the Kid! I saw your pictures on some 'Wanted' posters. I'm Tell Sackett."

They started to shake hands but were interrupted by the sudden arrival of yet another man through the curtain. He was dressed in a uniform and helmet with strange symbols. All four men drew their weapons. "Who are you?" demanded Jesse James. "Why are you dressed so funny and what is that thing you're pointing at us?"

The fourth man answered with quiet menace. "My name is Jok-Tar and this," he flourished the weapon, "is a laser gun. It's mostly for killing Martians, but I could make an exception in your case."

"Now hold on," placated Tell Sackett, "instead of fighting, why don't we see if we can get back to where we came from?"

"Look!" shouted Billy the Kid, pointing where the shimmering curtain used to be. There was nothing there now except empty air and saw grass.

"Well," shrugged Jesse James, "we may not be able to get back. Listen, we're all gun fighters—why don't we team up and take over this town?" That sounded like a good idea, and they started making plans.

While they were talking, similar plans were being made a short distance away. Three teenagers also were scheming to take over the town. They were dressed in commando outfits and wore kerchiefs tied around their legs, headbands, and sunglasses. Each one carried a hunting knife on his belt. The tallest one was saying, "They just don't treat us right. They'll be sorry."

"Yeah," said the oldest, "making all that fuss just because I helped steal a car!"

"Right," said the youngest, "I actually had to sneak out of the house tonight. They'll be sorry when we take over the town."

The other two nodded. "Let's go!" They started walking toward town and almost bumped into the three gunmen and the space alien. All the men immediately drew their weapons and waited for someone to make the first move. Jesse James laughed, "Look at those funny clothes. They must be friends of yours, Jok-Tar."

"They're no friends of mine," he answered grimly.

One of the punks sneered, "What's your name—Jock Strap?" His laugh was cut short by Jok-Tar's menacing look. He took a step backward and said nervously, "Who are you guys anyway?"

They gave their names, still holding their guns ready. The boy frowned, "What year do you think this is?"

"1839," answered the cowboys. But Jok-Tar said, "2033."

"It's 1988," the kid replied, "you must have come through some kind of time warp."

Jok-Tar noticed his companions' puzzled looks and explained, "It's when you travel through time but stay in the same place."

Tell Sackett shrugged, "Well, we're here now, and we're going to take over this town. You kids look tough—why don't you join us?"

After they put their weapons away and the boys taught the gunfighters a fancy handshake, they walked toward the town.

A committee was meeting in the town hall to plan for the upcoming rodeo. A lot of arguing was going on and not much planning. Mary and her daughter Kathy considered themselves aristocracy and rightful leaders. The rodeo queens, Lily and Millie Miller, didn't see it that way and resented their snobbery. The sisters sarcastically referred to the two as the "Queen" and the "Princess." The Miller girls were angry because the Princess didn't want to start the meeting until the two male rodeo stars arrived, saying the rodeo needed to be represented by men. "You never give us our due," they complained, "we're rodeo stars, too."

The sheriff and his deputy sided with the Queen and, to add to the confusion, the Queen's poodle kept growling and trying to bite everyone's leg. The two male rodeo stars finally arrived and the poodle transferred her attentions to them. Everyone was shouting at once when the gang burst through the door with their weapons drawn.

Jesse James snarled, "Get your hands up. Stay where you are and no one will get hurt. Drop your guns on the floor." As the teenagers gathered up the guns, he added, "We're taking over this town."

Lily said, "Well shoot, you don't need guns for that. It's about time we had a change of leaders."

Her sister agreed, "Yeah, it's not like it's organized or anything."

Tell Sackett smiled. "Well, in that case, you can put your hands down. Boys, put your guns away. It appears we're welcome here. And look at these lovely ladies!"

Soon each cowboy was paired with a lady. Jok-Tar went over to the Queen but stopped when the dog started growling at him. Jok-Tar took out his laser gun and adjusted the setting. "Oh, don't hurt my puppy!" the Queen pleaded.

"Don't worry," he said, "I'm just going to teach it some manners." The dog yelped as the weapon sounded but then walked over to its mistress, sat down at her right heel, and wagged its tail. "Oh, thank you, Mister," the Queen said, "you turned her into a nice puppy."

The townsmen didn't like this new competition for the ladies and moved to challenge the newcomers. They were stopped by the ladies, who said, "Now, we're all going to have to learn to get along, and we might as well start now."

The three teenagers were left out of all this interaction and didn't like it. "Wait a minute!" the oldest one said, "I thought we were going to do some fighting and killing."

The gunmen stepped forward menacingly, their hands on their weapons. The youngest kid said, "I think I hear my mommy calling," and the three turned and ran away.

"Well," said Jok-Tar, his arm around the Queen, "it looks like we have a happy ending."

"No," said Millie, "it looks like we have a happy beginning."

The End

This play contains several stereotypes—aggressive gunfighters, a menacing alien, hostile teenagers, snobbish aristocracy, and passive women who express some resentment but mostly function as prizes for the men. As the small scenes were being developed, I initiated discussions about stereotypes and suggested that the women also might want to take over the town. The students listened politely, took part in the discussions, and then developed the scenes as they had wanted to in the first place. Because this was their play, I let it happen.

In the first few days of this activity, I tried to persuade the girl who played the puppy to choose a human character, but she refused. After the play was performed, her mother, who had been in the audience, came to me with tears in her eyes. My first thought was that she was disappointed because her daughter had not had any lines to speak in the play. The mother told me that her daughter never before had taken part in any school activities or had spoken to anyone outside the family. She said she had been so pleased at how happy and excited her daughter had been about being in the play and that for the first time her daughter actually had begun to make friends. I was so pleased that I hadn't insisted on her playing a person and reminded myself of something I already knew: to always allow students to go at their own pace.

THE POWER OF STORYTELLING

TABLE 5.1 Grade-Level Guidelines: Point of View (POV)

	K-12	PK-2	3-5	6-12
Add-a-Sense			X	X
Point of View			X	X
Panel Point of View			X	X
Alibi Point of View	X			
Point of View Aside			X	X
Shadow Point of View			X	X
Jury Trial Point of View				X
Creative Dramatics Point of View			X	X

Afterword

My usual contact with students is 1 hour a day during a 1- to 3-week residency, and then I'm off to another school, leaving you with all the work. I am filled with admiration for all you teachers who provide a safe and stimulating environment for learning and continually look for ways to expand your teaching skills, despite the myriad nonteaching demands made on your time. Yours is truly a Herculean task, and you manage to do it with cheerfulness and grace. I hope this book will help you and give you some good ideas.

Thank you.

Glossary

Allegory A story in which a second underlying meaning is implied. Beast fables are simple allegories.

Aside A stage movement often used in melodramas. The actor speaks lines, then interrupts the play by moving toward the audience and speaking directly to them. The other characters do not "hear" or respond, and the action stops until the actor returns to position to resume the play.

Blocking (noun) The movements an actor makes on stage, whether planned or spontaneous.

(verb) Standing between an actor and the audience so that the audience cannot see the actor.

(verb) Preventing a scene from progressing by not accepting suggested changes.

Breaking character Stepping out of role by behaving or speaking in a way that one's character would not do.

Cast (noun) The actors in a play.

(verb) To select the actors for a play.

Charades A game in which teams pantomime song, movie, or book titles. The object is to guess the title in a certain length of time.

Circle story A story that begins and ends with the same line or situation.

Downstage (adjective or adverb) Toward the front of the stage and the audience. This term and *upstage* are remnants from a time when plays were performed on a raked stage, that is, one tilted so that the audience could see the actors better. The back of the stage was actually higher than the front, hence the use of *up* and *down* instead of *away* and *toward* or *back* and *front*. To further confuse matters, *right* and *left* refer to the actor's right and left when he or she is facing the audience, not to the audience's right or left.

Fable A brief story that ends in a moral lesson.

Fairy tale A story using stereotyped characters in magical and fanciful settings.

Fish story A story containing exaggerations but told as if it were true.

Focus (noun) The characters and action that the audience are watching. An actor can give or take focus.

(verb) To concentrate on what your character is thinking and feeling.

(verb) To concentrate on the action taking place.

Folktale A term used for any story handed down traditionally.

Legend An exaggerated folk tale often based on fact.

Leitmotif A musical theme that accompanies a character or situation.

Mime (noun) A performer who uses a stylized and exaggerated form of pantomime. Mimes often wear stylized makeup and costumes and usually work with few or no props.

Myth A fanciful explanation of natural phenomena.

Oral history Verbal reminiscences about the past that are usually tape-recorded and later transcribed.

Pantomime (verb) To act with or without props, without making any sound.

Parable A short story that ends with a moral lesson or demonstrates a spiritual value. The characters are usually human beings.

Props (noun) Short for *property*. Refers to any object used or worn on stage that has not been designated as costume, makeup, or part of the set.

Reader's theater A performance of a play with the actors reading from the script instead of speaking memorized lines. The actors usually sit in chairs or stand at lecterns, and movement is limited.

Round robin A storytelling activity in which students contribute consecutively to a story.

Run-through A rehearsal of a play in which the entire play is performed without stopping.

Scenario Outline of a plot, listing entrances, exits, and main actions. It may include a few key phrases of dialogue.

Set (noun) Movable or stationary scenery and furnishings that decorate the stage. If any of the objects are used by the actors except for entrances and exits, they usually are referred to as *props,* with the possible exception of mirrors and windows.

Shadow (verb) A dramatic device. An actor speaks and acts in character while a second actor immediately speaks and behaves as he or she thinks the character actually is feeling and thinking. The first actor tries to hide these inner thoughts from the other characters.

Tall tale A story often based on fact but wildly exaggerated.

Triad A group of three people.

Upstage (adjective) Toward the back of the stage, away from the audience.

(verb) Take focus away from another actor.

Urban legends Persistent stories that are told in many regions that are not true but are believed by many people.

Voice-over A spoken narrative that accompanies a film or slide show, also commonly used in commercials. The term also applies to the voices given to animated cartoons.

Work To rehearse a segment of a play intensively and repeatedly, trying various styles and variations.

Resources

Character Description Form, Simplified

Name of character _____

What does the character look like?

_____

Where does the character live?

_____

How does the character travel?

_____

How does the character spend his or her time?

_____

What does the character eat?

_____

What does the character want?

_____

What is the character afraid of?

_____

What does the character think of him- or herself?

_____

What do others think of the character?

_____

Does the character have any special powers?

_____

Comments:

_____
_____
_____

Character Description Form, Detailed

Name of character _____

Physical appearance (eyes, hair, build, height, distinguishing marks)
_____
_____
_____

Status (position in family, occupation, financial condition. What do others think of him or her? What does the character think of him- or herself? Ambitions?)
_____
_____
_____

Personality (attitudes, beliefs, philosophy, hopes, fears. Is the character greedy, nervous, loving, lazy?)
_____
_____
_____

Abilities (skills, magical powers, etc.)
_____
_____
_____

How does the character spend his or her time? (work, leisure, hobbies, responsibilities)
_____
_____
_____

Setting (location, time in history, type of home, means of travel, dress, foods, political atmosphere. Is there magic?)
_____
_____
_____

References

Aardema, V. (1960). *In West Africa*. New York: Cowerd McCann.

Barrie, J. M. (1980). *Peter Pan in Kensington Gardens*. Cutchogue, NY: Harmony Raine.

Beowulf (R. K. Gordon, Trans.). (1992). New York: Dover. (Original work published 1000)

Brunvand, J. H. (1981). *The vanishing hitchhiker: American urban legends and their meanings*. New York: Norton.

Brunvand, J. H. (1984). *The choking Doberman and other "new" urban legends*. New York: Norton.

Brunvand, J. H. (1989). *Curses, broiled again: The hottest urban legends going*. New York: Norton.

Day, A. (1990). *Carl's Christmas*. New York: Farrar, Strauss and Giroux.

Day, A. (1991a). *Carl's afternoon in the park*. New York: Farrar, Strauss and Giroux.

Day, A. (1991b). *Good dog, Carl*. New York: Farrar, Strauss and Giroux.

Day, A. (1992a). *Carl goes shopping*. New York: Farrar, Strauss and Giroux.

Day, A. (1992b). *Carl's masquerade*. New York, Farrar, Strauss and Giroux.

Day, A. (1993). *Carl goes to day care*. New York: Farrar, Strauss and Giroux.

Day, A. (1994). *Carl makes a scrapbook*. New York: Farrar, Strauss and Giroux.

Goodman, K. (1986). *What's whole in whole language?* Portsmouth, NH: Heinemann.

Hamilton, V. (1988). *In the beginning: Creation stories from around the world*. San Diego, CA: Harcourt Brace.

Ireland, N. O. (1989). *Index to fairy tales*. Westwood: Faxon.

Jonas, A. (1983). *Round trip*. New York: Greenwillow.

Jonas, A. (1985). *The trek*. New York: Greenwillow.

Lima, C., & Lima, J. (1989). *A to zoo: Subject access to children's picture books*. New York: Bowker.

Longfellow, H. W. (1983). *Hiawatha*. New York: Dial. (Original work published 1900)

Mayer, M. (1967). *Boy, a dog and a frog*. New York: Dial.

Mayer, M. (1968). *Frog, where are you?* New York: Dial.

Mayer, M. (1969). *One frog too many*. New York: Dial.

Spolin, V. (1963). *Improvisation for the theater*. Evanston: Northwestern University Press.

Van Allsburg, C. (1984). *The mysteries of Harris Burdick*. Boston: Houghton Mifflin.

Wilson, G., & Moss, J. (1988). *Books for children to read alone*. New York: Bowker.

Yaakov, J., & Greenfieldt, J. (1991). *Fiction catalog*. New York: H. W. Wilson.